Work in Progress

Course Book

Andy Hopkins
Jocelyn Potter

LONGMAN

Map of the book

Information for pairwork *page 137*   Tapescripts *page 140*

Introduction

Work in Progress is about people working in four different companies. Look at the pictures of the companies below.

1 Match each picture (A – D) with one on the opposite page (1 – 4).

2 Which company:
a sells things in a shop?
b makes things in a factory?
c tells people about the news?
d gives help and ideas to other companies?

3 🔊 Listen to the tape. Match each extract with one of the companies.

4 Match each company with one of these business areas:
- manufacturing
- media
- retail
- services

Use a dictionary to help you.

1

2

3

4

Customer Order

Music Stand

Name: P. Haines   Date: 26 / 2 / 97

Address: 45 Mill Road

Witney   Tel: 346 120

Item: Yamaha keyboard PSR 520

Price: £529.99   Deposit: £50

Shop talk

1

Music Stand

- Find out about a business
- Listen to an interview
- Listen to a conversation in a shop
- Buy and sell
- Grammar:
  have got

The busy town of Witney, population 25,000, lies ten miles from the city of Oxford. The main shopping area is in the centre of town, around High Street and Bridge Street.

Morag Findlay

Manager

Music Stand
62 High Street
Witney
Oxfordshire
OX8 6HJ
Tel: 01993 352445

Reading about a business

1 **Look at the pictures and the information above. Are these sentences true or false? Do we know? Correct the false information.**

a Music Stand is a music shop.
b The shop is in Oxford.
c It is in Bridge Street.
d It is in the town centre.
e It is closed now.
f Morag is a shop assistant.
g She sells books of music.

Listening and Reading: an interview

2 **Guess answers to these questions.**

a Why does Morag run a music shop?
b What does she sell?
c Which things are popular?
d Who are Morag's customers?
e When is the shop open?
f Are there other music shops in Witney?

3 **Listen and read. Check your answers to Exercise 2.**

Interviewer: Are you a musician?
Morag: Yes, music is really important to me. I'm a singer, my boyfriend's a musician, and a lot of our friends are in the music world.
Interviewer: What have you got in the shop?
Morag: We've got musical instruments – pianos, violins, guitars – and a lot of books and sheet music. I've always got popular instruments like recorders in the shop, but we can order anything.
Interviewer: And who are your customers?
Morag: Oh, adults, young people and children – people of all ages.
Interviewer: And when is the shop open?
Morag: Six days a week, between nine thirty and six. Witney has got a lot of shops but we're the only general music shop here.

Grammar: *have got*

4 **Find examples of *have got / has got* in the interview. Then complete these sentences with forms of *have got*.**

a Some customers have got a lot of money.
b ..... Morag ..... an assistant?
c ..... the instruments ..... price tags?
d This customer .... a new guitar.
e I ..... not ..... an answerphone in the shop.
f The shop ..... not ..... a fax number.

▶▶ p.12 **Grammar backup 1**

Listening to a conversation in the shop

5 **Listen to Morag and a customer. Which phrases do they use?**

a • Good morning.
  • Good afternoon.
  • Good evening.
b • behind the counter
  • in the back
  • on the shelf
c • £3.50
  • £35.00
  • £350.00
d • Cash.
  • By cheque.
  • By credit card.
e • Your receipt.
  • Your change.
  • Your bill.

6 **How do you reply to these phrases?**

a Good morning.
b Can I help you?
c Have you got a white Fender guitar?
d How much is it?
e How are you paying?
f Goodbye.

 Listen again to the conversation in Exercise 5 and check your answers.

Speaking: buying and selling

7 **Look at these pictures. Work with a partner. Use expressions from the Phrasebook.**

  A: You are a shop assistant.
  B: You are a customer. Buy one of the things in the pictures.

a calculator

a diary

a calendar

a cassette

Phrasebook

Asking for things

Have you got a guitar?
Can I have a recorder **please**?
I'd like some sheet music.
I'm looking for a piano.

Action | B

Working with numbers

- Understand and use numbers
- Understand and give prices
- Complete an order form

Listening to numbers

1 Look at the ticket for the British National Lottery.

a 🔊 Listen. How many numbers on the ticket are correct?

b 🔊 Write six numbers between 1 and 49. Listen. How many correct numbers have you got?

2 Name the objects in the pictures A – H. Choose words from the list.

EXAMPLES: *It's a credit card. They're price tags.*

| price tags | ticket | building | catalogue entry | computer |
| passports | telephone | credit card | | |

3 🔊 Listen. Match the numbers with the objects in Exercise 2. Then listen again and say the numbers.

Speaking: sharing information

4 **Work in pairs. You want to buy a car together and you have information about different cars.**

A: Turn to page 137.

B: Use the information below to answer your partner's questions. Then answer his/her questions.

Model:	Ford Escort
Age:	3 years
Price:	£4,995
Telephone Number:	0181 326 8876

When you finish, check your answers with your partner.

Listening to prices

5 Look at the pictures. Match the pictures with the items in the catalogue. Then listen and write the missing prices (A – E).

Music Stand

piano ....
guitar ....
keyboard ....
drum kit ....
harmonica ....
recorder ....
microphone ....
sheet music ....
music stand ....

Speaking: talking about prices

6 **Work in pairs. Ask and answer about the prices in the pictures above.**

EXAMPLE: *How much is this drum kit?*
It's seven hundred and sixty-eight pounds.

Listening and Writing: completing an order form

7 Listen.

a   What does the customer want to buy?

b   Has Morag got it?

Listen again. Complete an order form like the one on the right.

Customer Order   *Music Stand*

Name: __Alison Batey__   Date: __27.12.96__

Address: _____

_____   Tel: _____

Item: _____

Price: _____   Deposit: _____

Action **C**

Taking an order

- Spell names and addresses
- Give and take an order
- Vocabulary:
  - the alphabet
  - addresses
- Grammar:
  possessive adjectives

Listening and Speaking: the alphabet

1   Look at the letters of the alphabet on the left. Practise saying the letters in English.

2   🔊 Listen. Which is the correct spelling?

a Thomson	• Thompson	d Tennison	• Tennyson
b Hyde	• High	e Carter	• Harper
c Sheep	• Ship	f Fraser	• Frazer

Listening and Writing: names and addresses

3   🔊 Listen. In which order does each speaker say:

a   the house number and street name?

b   the town or city?

c   his or her name?

Listen again. Write the names and addresses.

Grammar: possessive adjectives

4   Complete the conversations with these words:

> my   your   his   her   its   our   their

Addresses

A B C D E F G H I J K L M N O P Q R S T U V W X Y Z

a   'Can I have your address, please?'
'Yes, ... address is 27 Bank Street.'
'Is the recorder for ..... daughter?'
'Yes, it's ..... birthday tomorrow.'
'Here's the recorder and ..... case. Do you want a bag?'
'No, thank you.'

b   'I know those people. What are ..... names?'
'..... name's John Fisher, and I think ..... name's Penny.'
'Ah! ..... house is in Bank Street. They live near ..... mother.'

 p.13   Grammar backup 1

Writing: names and addresses

5 Look at the addresses below.

a Find short forms that mean:
  • Street • Road • a man • a woman

b In each address, which is:
  • the first name? • the surname?
  • the house number? • the postcode?

c Write each address in the right order for an envelope.

d How are addresses different in your country?

A Ms Erica Mill
   Oxford OX2 3BJ
   229 Devon St.

B London W9 2PT
   11 Bridge Rd.
   Mr Peter Elmore

6 What are the full forms of the circled letters below? Use a dictionary to help you.

ACTION Music Co.

John Price

Action Music Co.
14 Tavistock Sq.
Edinburgh

Tel. 914223
Fax 914445

Frances Colton
Western Newspapers Ltd.
P.O. Box 235
Bristol

Catalogue no.	Price
002356	19.99
002357	25.49
002358	29.99

Speaking: giving and taking an order

7 Work in pairs. Give and take an order. Use expressions from the Phrasebook.

  A: Turn to page 137.
  B: You are a customer in a music shop and you want to buy an instrument.

> *Phrasebook*
>
> **Spelling**
>
> **How do you spell** Taylor?
> **Can you spell** your name **for me?**
> **That's** T-O-N-I.
> **It's spelt** M-O-R-A-G.
> **It's** Sarah **with** an 'h'.

Talking point

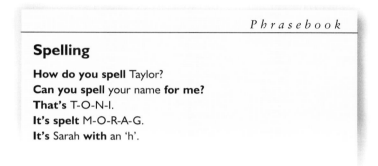

THE CUSTOMER IS ALWAYS RIGHT!

What do *you* think?

Word file Unit 1		
SHOPS	guitar	street
bill	harmonica	surname
buy	instrument	telephone number
cash	keyboard	
catalogue	microphone	**OFFICE**
change	music stand	**SUPPLIES**
cheque	musician	calculator
closed	piano	calendar
credit card	recorder	computer
customer	sheet music	diary
deposit	singer	
in stock		**OTHER**
manager	**ADDRESSES**	building
open	company	cassette
order	fax number	passport
price tag	first name	ticket
receipt	house number	
sell	limited	
shop assistant	P.O. Box	
	postcode	
MUSIC	road	
drum kit	square	

Grammar *backup 1*

have got

Practice

1 Complete the sentences with a form of *have got*.

a Morag *has got* a shop in Witney.
b She ..... not ..... a fax machine.
c Young people ..... not ..... a lot of money.
d '..... Witney ..... a lot of shops?'
  'Yes, it ..... .'
e 'Excuse me, ... you ..... a book of children's songs?'
  'No, I'm sorry, we ..... .'

2 Look at the picture. Imagine you are going on a trip. Your friend is looking at your packing list. Write his questions and your short answers.

EXAMPLE: *'Have you got your passport?'*
'Yes, I have.'

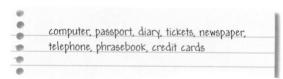

computer, passport, diary, tickets, newspaper, telephone, phrasebook, credit cards

3 Write the full forms.

a We haven't got time. *We have not got time.*
b I've got a price list.
c I think he's got a new address.
d The guitar's got a red case.
e She hasn't got a catalogue.
f The computer's got a price tag.

4 Translation

Write these sentences in your own language.

a Has she got a good job?
b We've got a new office.
c They haven't got a telephone.

Reference

We use **have / has (not) got** to talk about possession.

Statements

I You We They	've have (not) haven't	got a calculator.
He She It	's has (not) hasn't	

Questions

Have	I you we they	got a computer?
Has	he she it	

Short answers

Yes,	I you we they	have.
	he she it	has.
No,	I you we they	haven't/have not.
	he she it	hasn't/has not.

It is common in speech and informal writing to use short forms.

I**'ve got** ...
She **hasn't got** ...

In formal writing we use the full forms.

I **have got** ...
She **has not got** ...

Possessive adjectives: *my, your, his, her, its, our, their*

Practice

1 Complete the sentences with a possessive adjective.

a What's *your* address, please?
b Your sister – what's ..... name?
c John and Sue want a bicycle for ..... son.
d The new shop? ..... customers are all young people.
e We've got a problem. ..... new assistant is ill.

2 Look at the pictures. Complete the sentences with possessive adjectives.

a Excuse me, is that *your* suitcase?
b I think that's ..... card.
c I'm sorry. I think that's ..... seat.
d I think that's ..... dog.
e ..... seats are here.

Reference

We use possessive adjectives to answer the question **Whose ...?**

EXAMPLE: **Whose** *office is that?*
It's **our** *office.*

Possessive adjectives come before a noun.

EXAMPLES: ***my name***
her address

pronoun	possessive adjective
I	**my**
you	**your**
he	**his**
she	**her**
it	**its**
we	**our**
they	**their**

3 Translation

Write these sentences in your own language.

a Their friends have got a restaurant in Marseilles.
b Their friend is a famous guitarist.

Open for business

2

- Read and write messages
- Tell the time
- Vocabulary:
  - office supplies
- Grammar:
  - imperatives
  - prepositions of time

Take note

Reading messages

1 Read the messages and find words for items A – F and actions G – J.

Message `1`

From: Bank Manager
For: Morag
Please phone him.
Rachel

Time: 2.15 p.m.
Date: Friday

Sara
Important meeting between 3.00 and 4.00 p.m. Please stop all calls. `2`

There's a problem with the lights in the photocopier room. Please call an electrician as soon as possible. `3`

`7` Don't forget!
The new sales assistant starts tomorrow morning at 9.45.

Things to do on Monday:
send the package to Hungary (DHL?)
fax the report to Oslo `6`

I'm in Paris on Friday. Please cancel the 11.30 meeting with Ms Sellars and find another time. `5`

Please buy: `4`
- fax rolls (10)
- printer ribbons (5)
- envelopes (1000)

Invitation
To ....Morag & Pete..........
From ....Barbara................

Please come to a party at
..........my house............
on ....Sat. March 12th........
at .....9 p.m................. `8`

2 Read the messages again. Which messages ask the reader to:
a telephone someone?
b send something?
c buy something?
d come to a party?
e welcome someone?
f stop something?
g take immediate action?

Grammar: imperatives

3 Look at the messages again. Find sentences with the word *please*.

a Look at the verbs that come after *please*. Which verb form is correct in this instruction?
   Please opening / open / opens / opened those letters.

b Find a negative instruction in the messages.

c Make the instruction in (a) negative.

4 Complete each sentence with the verb in brackets.

a *Meet* me at six o'clock. (meet)

b ..... in the morning. I'm working. (not / come)

c .....! There's a party this evening. (not / forget)

d ..... her tomorrow. She's out today. (call)

e This report's late. Please ..... it today. (finish)

 p.20 **Grammar backup 2**

Listening and Speaking: telling the time

5 Look at the clock.

Now look at these clocks. Write the time for each clock.

a   b   c

6   Listen and write the times you hear. Do you talk about time in the same way in your language?

P h r a s e b o o k

Asking the time

What's the time?
What time is it?
Have you got the time, please?

7 Work in pairs. Ask and answer questions about the time.

   A: Turn to page 137.
   B: Ask your partner about the times of:

   • the party   • the film

   EXAMPLE: *What time is the train?*
                  At quarter past three.

   Write the answers. Then answer your partner's questions with this information:

   • bus: 4.25   • meeting: 9.10

Writing messages

8 Study the expressions in the Phrasebook below. Write the messages. Use the correct prepositions.

a meet me / 3.00 / Sunday
   Please meet me at three o'clock on Sunday.

b call me / 9.00 / morning

c phone me / 2.30 / Monday afternoon

d don't call me / 11.00–12.00 / Thursday morning

e fax me / Tuesday

f send the package / Monday afternoon

g come / 9.00 / evening

h open the shop / 8.30 / Saturday

 p.20 **Grammar backup 2**

P h r a s e b o o k

Times of day

The meeting's **at half past four.**
Call me **between three and four o'clock.**
See me **in the morning.**
Send the report **on Friday.**
Fax him **on Tuesday morning.**
Meet me **on Wednesday afternoon.**

Action **B**

Learning the job

- Find out about a Saturday job
- Give instructions
- Write messages
- Vocabulary:
  - office furniture and equipment
  - shop tasks
  - days of the week

Vocabulary: office furniture and equipment

1 Match each picture (A – M) with a word from the box. Use a dictionary to help you.

> counter desk cupboard till shelves filing cabinet
> credit card machine security camera chair table
> computer printer fax machine

2 Group the words under these headings.

equipment	furniture
computer	chair

3 Think of an office or a shop that you know. List the equipment and furniture there.

Vocabulary: shop tasks

4 Look at this list of words. Complete each sentence with a verb from the list. Use a dictionary to help you.

> make unpack lock take put clean order open

a ..... prices on the books.
b ..... the money to the bank.
c ..... new instruments from the manufacturer.
d ..... the door at the end of the day.
e ..... the shop in the morning.
f ..... money from the customers.
g ..... the boxes.
h ..... money in the till.
i ..... tea and coffee for the staff.
j ..... the floor and the windows.

Reading about a Saturday job

5 Which tasks in Exercise 4 are for a new young assistant at the Music Stand? Why not the others? Would you like to do this job?

6 Read about Morag's Saturday assistant and check your answers to Exercise 5.

> Saturday is our busy day, so we have a Saturday boy, Ben, to help us. He only works on Saturdays because he's still at school. He does a lot of the physical work – you know, he cleans the floor, makes tea and coffee, puts prices on the books and instruments. It's good to have an extra person on the till to take money from customers. There are a lot of boxes to unpack on Saturdays. Ben does that too.

Speaking: opening times

7 Look at these opening times for different businesses in Britain.

a Which day:
   • is after Monday?
   • is the day before the weekend?
b Which days:
   • are the weekend?
   • are weekdays?
   • are shops and businesses often closed?
c Are opening times the same in your country?
   If not, how are they different?

A

Clayton's
Department Store

Monday 10 a.m. – 6 p.m.
Tuesday 9 a.m. – 6 p.m.
Wednesday 9 a.m. – 6 p.m.
Thursday 9 a.m. – 8 p.m.
Friday 9 a.m. – 6 p.m.
Saturday 9 a.m. – 6 p.m.
Sunday CLOSED

B

NORTHERN Bank

Open for Business
Weekdays 9.30 – 3.30

C

Family
Minimarkets

Mon – Sat 8 a.m. – 8 p.m.
Sunday 8 a.m. – 2 p.m.

Vocabulary: days of the week

8 Look at the opening times for Clayton's. Listen and repeat the days of the week. Where is the main stress on each word?

Speaking and Listening: giving instructions

9 Look at the pictures on the right. Morag is telling Ben how to use the till. Match her instructions (a–h) with the pictures (A–H).

a Put the money in. Twenties here, tens there ...
b Give the receipt to the customer with the change.
c Press the buttons for each item.
d Don't leave your key in the till.
e Unlock the till with your key.
f Press the TOTAL button and the drawer opens.
g Don't leave the till open. Always close it.
h Take out the change.

10 Now listen to Morag. Put the instructions in the right order.

EXAMPLE: *1. Unlock the till with your key.*

11 Choose one of these pieces of equipment and tell your partner how to use it.

   • a fax machine
   • a video recorder
   • a photocopier

Here are some words to help you.

press	put (in)	put (down)	take (out)	start	stop	open
close	paper	video cassette	button	lid	glass	

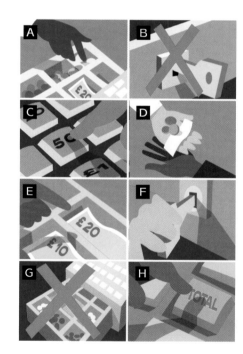

Writing messages

12 Write messages with instructions to a secretary. Use the messages on page 14 to help you.

a You have a meeting in your diary for 2.00 p.m. on Tuesday in Berlin, but you are in Frankfurt on that day.
b You want 500 more business cards.
c You want to leave the office early. Your secretary has a key. It is important that she gives the key to the security guard.

Action C

Working lives

- Describe jobs
- Ask about jobs
- Vocabulary:
  - places of work
  - work patterns
- Grammar:
  present simple

Reading about working lives

1 **Read the texts about three different jobs. Where does each person work?**

Paula Gonzalez is a student, but she has a part-time evening job as a receptionist in a night club in Buenos Aires.

When do the customers arrive?
'Our customers are usually tourists – they come at about 9.00 to see the tango show.'

What time do you start?
'I come to work at 8.00 every night of the week. The show starts at 10.00 and finishes a little after midnight.'

Do you like your job?
'Yes, I like the job. I meet people and I use my languages. I eat here after the customers leave, and I get home at about 1.00 a.m.'

Mercedes Sotelo works in a travel agency in Almeria in Spain. She has a full-time job but her day is in two parts. The office opens between 8.00 a.m. and 1.00 p.m. Then it opens again at 5.00 p.m. and closes at 7.00 p.m. 'It's about half an hour from the house to my office. It's a very long day, and I work on Saturday too.'

Riccardo Pavese works in a factory in Italy. He works shifts. One week he works in the mornings between 6.00 a.m. and 2.00 p.m., the next week he does afternoons, from 2.00 p.m. to 10.00 p.m. Then he works the night shift. This starts at 10.00 p.m. and finishes at 6.00 a.m. 'I'm single, so the shifts are OK. I don't work at the weekend. I see my friends then.'

2 **Now answer these questions.**

a Which people work full-time?
b Which people work on Saturdays?
c Which people meet different people every day?
d Who leaves work in the middle of the working day?
e Who eats after midnight?
f Who only works in the daytime?

3 **Write a list of six other places where people work.**

4 **Read these five sentences about work. Are they true or false?**

a If you work shifts, you work at different times of the day or night.
b Factory workers sell things to customers.
c A part-time job is an eight-hour day every day.
d Travel agencies sell tickets for visits to other countries.
e Receptionists sell food and drinks.

Speaking: work patterns

5 **Discuss the advantages and disadvantages of these different work patterns. Make lists.**

a • a full-time job   • a part-time job
b • a day job   • a night job
c • shift work   • regular office hours

EXAMPLE:

	ADVANTAGES	DISADVANTAGES
full-time job	good money	not much spare time

Say which work pattern you prefer and why.

Grammar: present simple

6 Read the texts in Exercise 1 again. Find verbs in the three texts that describe regular events.

EXAMPLE: *works*

When do these verbs end in *-s* or *-es*?

7 Read the sentences below. Complete each sentence with *work* or *works*.

a Riccardo works shifts.
b Paula ..... at night.
c Riccardo and Mercedes ..... full-time.
d Paula and I ..... in Buenos Aires.
e You ..... in Britain, don't you?
f I ..... part-time.

8 Read this interview. Put the words in the questions in the correct order.

a do / you / What / do / ?
   I'm a technician.
b you / Where / work / do / ?
   In a factory.
c full-time / Do / work / you / ?
   Yes, I do.
d you / Do / your job / like / ?
   Yes, it's OK.

 p.21   **Grammar backup 2**

Speaking: describing jobs

9 Work in pairs.

A: Turn to page 137.
B: Ask questions about your partner's job and complete the notes below. Use expressions from the Phrasebook. Then answer your partner's questions with your information.

A	B
job?	musician
place?	pubs
full-time?	no
start?	8.00 p.m.
finish?	11.00 p.m.
weekends?	yes
like job?	yes

Writing: describing a job

10 Write a paragraph about your partner's job. Use your notes from Exercise 9.

Phrasebook

Asking about jobs

What's your job?
What do you do?
Where do you work?

Talking point

I MAKE ALL MY TELEPHONE CALLS FROM WORK. THE BOSS DOESN'T KNOW, SO THAT'S OK.

What do *you* think?

Word file   Unit 2

FURNITURE / EQUIPMENT
chair
counter
credit card
   machine
cupboard
desk
fax machine
filing cabinet
photocopier
printer
security camera
shelf / shelves
table
till
video recorder

OFFICE SUPPLIES
envelope
fax roll
package
printer ribbon
report
video cassette

DAYS OF THE WEEK
Monday

Tuesday
Wednesday
Thursday
Friday
Saturday
Sunday
weekday
weekend

VERBS FOR INSTRUCTIONS
call
cancel
clean
close
fax
finish
forget
give
leave
(un)lock
meet
press
put
put down
put in
send
start
stop

take
take out
telephone / phone
unpack

TELLING THE TIME
half past
o'clock
quarter past / to

PLACES OF WORK
factory
night club
travel agency

WORKING PATTERNS
full-time
part-time
shift

OTHER
button
glass
key
lid
welcome

Grammar backup 2

Imperatives

Practice

1 Look at the pictures. Use the verbs in brackets to complete these instructions.

a Please *wash* your hands. (wash)
b ..... into this room. (go)
c ..... this water. (drink)
d Please ..... in this room. (smoke)
e Please ..... your name here. (sign)
f Please ..... this door. (open)

Reference

We use imperatives for orders and instructions (but not normally for requests).

Positive

Press the button.
Please **call** me at 10.00 a.m.
Write me a note.

Negative

Do not / don't open the shop before 9.30 a.m.
Do not / don't leave the office.
Please **do not / don't forget.**

2 Translation

Write these sentences in your own language.

a Open the shop.
b Unlock the till.
c Don't leave the keys in the door.
d Please don't use the telephone.

Prepositions of time

Practice

1 Write the time in words.

a 10.15 It's quarter past ten.
b 7.30
c 5.05
d 11.35

2 Write full sentences.

a Meet me / 6.00.
Meet me at six o'clock.
b Send the fax / the morning.
c Order the new computer / Tuesday.
d Come to my house / 5.45.

Reference

Time prepositions answer the question **When ...?**

at eight o'clock
ten **past** six
quarter **to** eleven
on Friday
in the morning
on Tuesday evening

3 Translation

Write these sentences in your own language.

a It's twenty past five.
b Phone me in the morning.
c I've got a meeting on Thursday.
d I arrive at work at half past eight.

Present simple

Practice

1 Complete these paragraphs with correct verb forms and prepositions.

a Emil *works* in a bookshop in Berlin. He ..... work ..... 8.30 ..... the morning and he .... 6 p.m.

b Pia ..... at a fitness centre. She ..... the evening shift. She ..... at the centre at 6 o'clock ..... the evening. She .... half past eleven.

c Richard and Sally ..... in a factory. They ..... their jobs very much.

2 Read this extract from an interview and write the interviewer's questions.

INTERVIEWER: What's your name?
MARK: Mark Hobday.
INTERVIEWER: (a) *Where do you live?* (live)
MARK: 44 Corn Street.
INTERVIEWER: Right. (b).....? (do)
MARK: I'm a manager of a small company.
INTERVIEWER: I see. Are you married?
MARK: Yes I am.
INTERVIEWER: (c).....? (wife / work)
MARK: Yes, she's a manager of the company too.
INTERVIEWER: (d) .....? (have got / children)
MARK: Yes, we've got two. They're not at home now, though.
INTERVIEWER: (e).....? (do)
MARK: Our son's at university and Juliet, our daughter, is a singer.

3 Write short answers.

a Does he work in a bank? (no)
 No, he doesn't.
b Do you like her? (yes)
c Do people smoke here? (no)
d Does she live near her work? (no)
e Does he play tennis? (yes)

4 Translation

Write these sentences in your own language.

a What does he do?
b They don't like night shifts.
c It opens at nine.
d When do you eat?

Reference

We use the present simple for routine actions and permanent situations.

Positive statements

I/You/We/They	work.
He/She/It	works.

Negative statements

I/You We/They	don't do not	work.
He/She/It	doesn't does not	

Questions

Do	I/you we/they	work?
Does	he/she/it	

Short answers

Yes,	I/you/we/they	do.
	he/she/it	does.
No,	I/you/we/they	don't/do not.
	he/she/it	doesn't/does not.

AND WHAT DOES YOUR HUSBAND DO?

Describing products

3

- ■ Understand an invoice
- ■ Describe where products are from
- ■ Vocabulary:
    countries and nationalities
- ■ Grammar:
    countable and
    uncountable nouns

World markets

Reading an invoice

1 Look at this invoice.

		Weber			Musikinstrumente Musical Instruments

J.A. Weber – Postfach 201967   D-80711 Munich (Germany)

Taylor James The Music Showroom The Plaza Swindon SN1 8PT G.B.		Acct no. 36015	Date 21/9/96	Order no. 026270
		Invoice No. 6870		

	Model no.	Description	Quantity	Unit price	Amount
01	3420	Cello	2	1350,00	2700,00

a Where do Weber instruments come from?
b What is the name of the English company on the invoice?

Listening to an interview

2 🔊 Listen and read.
a Which countries in Asia does Rachel mention?
b Which European countries does she mention?

Interviewer: The instruments you sell in the shop: where do they come from?
Rachel: Most of the keyboards and digital pianos, anything electronic comes from Japan or Korea. The guitars, again, come from Japan, Korea, Indonesia. We have a few German products, the Hohner harmonicas, and some of the, sort of, classical instruments like violins come from Germany, but, again, they're more expensive.
   Another country that's very cheap for production now is Romania and there are some Romanian violins and Hungarian violins and cellos. The pianos we sell ... the expensive ones are British, but again the cheaper ones are Chinese or Korean. So we do have a wide range of countries that manufacture the things that we sell.

COUNTRY	NATIONALITY
	-n, -ian
Argentina	Argentinian
Belgium	.....
Brazil	.....
Germany	.....
Hungary	.....
Indonesia	.....
Italy	.....
Korea	.....
Romania	.....
Russia	.....
USA	.....
	-ese
China	Chinese
Japan	.....
Vietnam	.....
	-ish
Britain	British
Poland	.....
Spain	.....
Sweden	.....
France	French
Switzerland	Swiss
.....	.....
.....	.....
.....	.....

3 Use information from the interview to complete the sentences.
a Electronic pianos come from Japan or ..... .
b Indonesia makes ..... .
c Hohner products are made in ..... .
d An example of a classical instrument is a ..... .
e Violins from ..... are cheap but violins from ..... are expensive.
f The pianos come from ....., ... and ..... .

Vocabulary: countries and nationalities

4 Complete the chart on the left, and add three other countries. Use a dictionary to help you.

Speaking: asking where products are from

5 **Work in pairs. Look at the map on the right.**

a Ask and answer about the products on the map.

EXAMPLE: *Where are Olivetti computers from?*
They're from Italy. They're Italian.

b Ask and answer about other products you know.

P h r a s e b o o k

Asking where products are from

Where's it from?
Where do they come from?
Where's it made?

Grammar: countable and uncountable nouns

6 **Look at the regular plural forms of these nouns.**
What rules can you make about nouns that have
***-es* and *-ies* endings?**

book – book<u>s</u>	address – address<u>es</u>	diary – diar<u>ies</u>
shop – shop<u>s</u>	watch – watch<u>es</u>	factory – factor<u>ies</u>
letter – letter<u>s</u>	dish – dish<u>es</u>	party – part<u>ies</u>

7 **Spell the plural forms of these nouns.**

a company *companies* e match
b drum   f nationality
c boss   g shop
d evening   h university

8 **Uncountable nouns are things we cannot count.**
They have no plural forms. Look at the pictures.

a Can you count water? b Can you count books?

9 **Look at the list below. Are these things countable**
or uncountable?

oil	taxi	photocopier	sugar	telephone
electricity	cotton	piano	music	money
dollar	apple	wine		

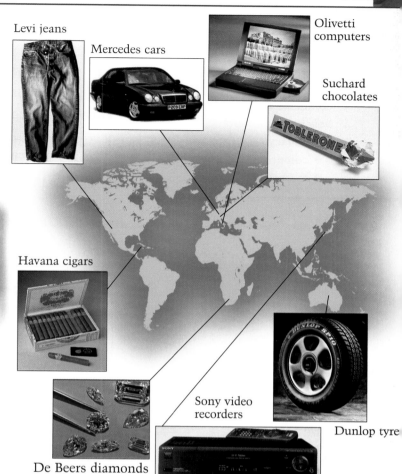

Levi jeans
Mercedes cars
Olivetti computers
Suchard chocolates
Havana cigars
Sony video recorders
Dunlop tyre
De Beers diamonds

10 **Study these sentences. When do we use *a / an*,**
some and *any*? Complete the chart.

I've got a pen, but I haven't got any paper. Have you
got any pieces of paper?
We've got some money but we haven't got any
dollars. Have you got a dollar?

	✓ positive	✗ negative	? question
+singular noun		a	
+plural noun	some		
+uncountable noun			any

▶▶ p.28 Grammar backup 3

Speaking: asking questions

11 **Work in pairs.**
A: Turn to page 137.
B: You want to buy these things at a music shop.

• guitar strings • violin case • CDs
• songbooks • cassette recorder

Ask the shop assistant for them.

EXAMPLE: *Have you got any guitar strings?*
Yes, we have. / I'm sorry. We haven't.

It's your choice

- Complete an order form
- Describe a product
- Vocabulary:
  - colours
  - materials

Vocabulary: colours

1 🔊 Look at the picture below. Match the objects and colours. Listen to a telephone conversation and check your answers.

COLOURS:	black	green	red	blue	yellow	white
	brown	grey	purple	pink		
OBJECTS:	carpet	walls	door	sofa	shelves	desk	phone
	chairs	tables	drum kit				

Talking point

I THINK GREY IS A GOOD COLOUR FOR OFFICES. OFFICES ARE FOR WORK NOT FOR HAVING FUN.

What do *you* think?

2 Describe the man's office. Write about the colours of the objects in the picture.

EXAMPLES: *The shelves are pink. He's got a white phone.*

3 Work in pairs. Ask and answer about colours in your office or a room at home.

EXAMPLES: *What colour is the carpet? It's green.*
What colour are the chairs? They're grey.

Vocabulary: materials

4 Match each word with a picture (A – E). Use a dictionary to help you.

| wool | cotton | silk | leather | denim |

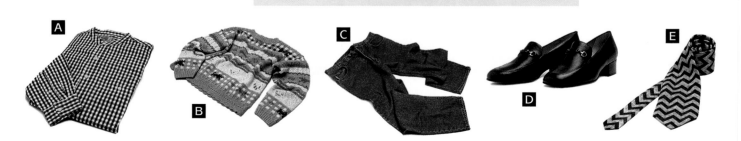

What other products are made from these materials?

Listening to a telephone order

5 🔊 **Listen. The manager of a clothes shop is ordering from a wholesaler. Complete the order form below.**

ORDER FORM

	COLOUR	MATERIAL	PRICE	QUANTITY
Shirts	green	silk	£29.99	20
Jackets				
Jumpers				
Shoes				
Jeans				
Trousers				

Speaking: describing products

6 **Look at the materials and the pictures below. Match the objects A – H with the materials in the box.**

> glass   leather   plastic   vinyl   metal
> wood   clay   rubber

7 **Look at this paragraph about the tyre.**

> It's a black tyre. It's made in Australia by Dunlop. The tyre is made of rubber and the middle is made of metal.

a Which of the expressions below comes before:
   • a material?   • a place?   • a company?
   It's made in .....
   It's made by .....
   It's made of .....

b Work in pairs. Choose one of the other products in the pictures. Describe it to your partner.

Writing: describing objects

8 **Choose an object in the room or in your office. Write a paragraph about it. Describe the colour and say where it is from, which company makes it and what the materials are.**

Speaking: describing objects

9 **Work in pairs.**

   A: Your partner is thinking of an object. What is it? Ask questions to find out about it. Your partner can only answer *Yes* or *No*.

   EXAMPLES: *Is it red?*
                   Is it made of wood?
                   Is it made by a Japanese company?

   B: Think of an object. Answer your partner's questions. You can only answer *Yes* or *No*.

- Describe present activities
- Understand and complete a customs form
- Grammar:
  present continuous

Doing the job

Reading about work in progress

1 Read the text. Name the people in each of the photographs (A – C).

> Pete is Morag's partner, but he doesn't work in the Music Stand. He's got his own business and workshop in a small town near Witney. He renovates good quality pianos and cellos. He buys old instruments and repairs or rebuilds them.
>
> 'My son, Jamie, is with me today. We're working on different jobs at the moment. I'm rebuilding a piano. It's German, made in about 1910. Right now I'm painting the metal frame. Jamie's working on a cello bow.
>
> I also visit people's homes and tune their pianos, but I'm not doing that today. I'm staying in the workshop.'

2 Read this information about Pete and Jamie. Is it true or false?
a Pete works in Witney.
b He works in a workshop.
c He sells new instruments.
d He is repairing a British piano.
e His son is not working with him today.
f Pete sometimes tunes pianos.
g He is tuning a piano today.

Grammar: present continuous

3 Find verbs in the text that refer to:
a regular activities (present simple verbs).
b present activities (present continuous verbs).

4 Complete the chart with present continuous forms of *work*.

I	.....		
He She It	.....	(not)	.....
You We They	.....		

5 Add *not* to make these sentences negative.
a I am writing a book.
b She is waiting for you.
c The train is coming.
d They are having a meeting.

6 Look at the picture below. Write short answers to these questions.

EXAMPLES: *Yes, he is. No, she isn't.*

a Is Teresa making tea?
b Is Brian sending a fax?
c Is the computer working?
d Are John and Sally shaking hands?

 p.29 **Grammar backup 3**

Speaking about present activities

7 Work in pairs. Ask and answer questions.

A: Turn to page 138.
B: There are six differences between the picture on this page and your partner's picture. Ask and answer questions about the people in the picture to find the differences.

EXAMPLE: *Is Alan sweeping the floor?*
No, he isn't. He's ...

Writing: completing a customs form

8 Look at the customs form.

a How many kilos is the box?
b What is in it?
c Are they a gift?

9 Choose a gift for a friend in another country. Work in pairs. Ask your partner about his / her gift and complete the customs form below for it.

CUSTOMS
May be opened officially

Detailed description of contents	Value (Customs) (specify the currency)
2 cotton T-shirts. One large and green. One small and black.	£15

Net Weight 1.5 kg | Total value £15

☐ Gift ☑ Merchandise

I certify that this item does not contain any dangerous article prohibited by postal regulations.

Signature ...... *G. Marsh*

CUSTOMS
May be opened officially

Detailed description of contents	Value (Customs) (specify the currency)

Net Weight | Total value

☐ Gift ☐ Merchandise

I certify that this item does not contain any dangerous article prohibited by postal regulations.

Signature ......

Word file   Unit 3

COLOURS	plastic	customs form
black	rubber	expensive
blue	silk	gift
brown	vinyl	made by
green	wood	made in
grey	wool	made of
pink		manufacture
purple	**CLOTHES**	nationality
red	jacket	paint
white	jeans	rebuild
yellow	jumper	renovate
	shirt	repair
MATERIALS	shoes	stay
clay	tie	tune
cotton	trousers	visit
denim		workshop
glass	**OTHER**	
leather	cheap	
metal	country	

Countable and uncountable nouns

Practice

1 Countable (C) or uncountable (U)?

- shop *C*
- assistant
- customer
- money
- ticket
- equipment
- deposit
- till
- tea
- coffee
- cup of tea
- fax

2 Complete these sentences with *a, some* or *any*.

a We're putting *some* new furniture in that room.
b Would you like ..... cup of coffee?
c I haven't got ..... money.
d She's got ..... ticket to Madrid.
e There aren't ..... violin books.
f Would you like to leave ..... deposit?
g Have you got ..... harmonicas?

3 Look at the picture. What is in the woman's briefcase?

EXAMPLE: *She's got some keys.*

4 Translation
    Write these sentences in your own language.

a I'd like some coffee.
b Have we got any sugar?
c She doesn't want any gifts.

Reference

Countable nouns

Countable nouns refer to things you can count.

EXAMPLES: *one book, three books; one person, three people*

Uncountable nouns

Uncountable nouns refer to things you cannot count.

EXAMPLES: *water, music, air*

Plural forms of regular, countable nouns

Most nouns add an **-s** for the plural.

EXAMPLES: *town**s**, name**s**, bag**s***

Nouns ending in **s**, **ss**, **sh**, **ch** and **x** add **-es** in the plural.

EXAMPLES: *bus**es**, boss**es**, box**es***

Nouns ending in consonant + **y** have a plural form ending in **-ies.**

EXAMPLES: *count**ries**; party – part**ies***

a / some / any

We use **a** before singular countable nouns. (We use **an** before singular countable nouns that begin with a vowel).

EXAMPLES: *I'm not **a** manager. I'm **a** secretary.*
          *Are you **a** secretary too?*

We use **some** before plural countable nouns when we do not want to be exact about the number.

EXAMPLE: *I've got **some tickets** for the play tonight.*

We also use **some** before uncountable nouns.

EXAMPLE: *We've got **some milk** in the fridge.*

We usually use **any** in questions and negative sentences before plural countable nouns and uncountable nouns.

EXAMPLES: *Have you got **any black pens**?*
          *We haven't got **any time**.*

Present continuous

Practice

1 **Look at the diary and the pictures from the security cameras. What are people really doing in these rooms?**

EXAMPLE: *Room 1 – They aren't having a meeting. They're having a party!*

September	27th
Room 1 – meeting	Room 3 – closed for cleaning
Room 2 – interview	Room 4 – meeting

Room 1 Room 2

Room 3

Room 4

2 **Write questions using present continuous forms.**

a what / you / do?
  What are you doing?
b where / Jane / study?
c why / we / wait?
d where / you / go?
e they / have / meeting?
f the man / repair / the photocopier?

3 **Complete these sentences with the correct forms of the verbs. Choose a present continuous or a present simple form.**

a I usually *work* (work) from 9.00 a.m. to 5.00 p.m. but today I *am working* (work) until midnight.
b Ms Young ..... (have) a meeting at the moment and I'm afraid her secretary ..... (have) lunch.
c We always ..... (sell) a lot of woollen clothes in winter.
d Morag usually ..... (stay) in her shop all day, but Pete often ..... (visit) customers' houses. Today he ..... (tune) a piano in Oxford.

4 **Translation**

Write these sentences in your own language.

a He's using the computer at the moment.
b Where are you going?
c We're all working hard this week.

Reference

We use the present continuous to refer to present activities: activities that are happening now and that are not finished.

Positive statements

I	'm/am	
He/She/It	's/is	going.
You/We/They	're/are	

Negative statements

I	'm not/am not	
He/She/It	isn't/is not	waiting.
You/We/They	aren't/are not	

Questions

	am	I	
(Where)	is	he/she/it	working?
	are	you/we/they	

Short answers

		I	am.
Yes,		he/she/it	is.
		you/we/they	are.
		I	'm not/am not.
No,		he/she/it	isn't/is not.
		you/we/they	aren't/are not.

People and jobs

4

The right job?

- Describe jobs
- Understand job advertisements
- Listen to a job interview
- Describe skills and interests
- Vocabulary:
  - adjectives to describe jobs
  - skills
- Grammar:
  - *can / can't*
  - *like / enjoy + -ing*

Discussion: jobs

1 **What do you think these people do in their jobs?**
   - the assistant to a bank manager
   - the marketing manager of an airline
   - the personal assistant to a famous musician
   - an interpreter for a politician
   - a receptionist in the head office of a multinational company
   - a secretary in a newspaper company
   - the manager of a CD shop

2 **Look at the pictures below. Use the adjectives to say what you think about the jobs above.**

   EXAMPLE: the assistant to a bank manager:
   I think it's an interesting job.
   I think it's very boring.

boring / dull

fun

interesting

exciting frightening / terrifying

relaxing

3 **What other jobs can you describe with these adjectives? Discuss them with your partner.**

Reading job advertisements

4 **Read the job advertisements on the left.**

Which job:	Which jobs:
a is in a shop?	e are in capital cities?
b is in a newspaper office?	f involve selling things?
c is in a radio station?	g interest you? Why?
d involves travel?	

A

ail No. aston@enterpr....net

ADMINISTRATIVE ASSISTANT

required for EURO-FM radio station. Exciting opportunity for the right person. Apply to: Monica Dupres, P.O. Box 1342, Amsterdam, The Netherlands

B

SALES ASSISTANT

at MAYHEM MODE in central London. Fashion clothes and accessories. Good salary and conditions. Please apply in writing to: Mr R. Kumar, Mayhem Mode, 45 Oxford Street, London WIP 3SH.

SENIOR SECRETARY

in international Advertising Dept. of newspaper group based in Paris. Languages and good secretarial skills essential. Some travel. Personnel Manager, 21 Ave. Charles I, 75003 Paris.

C

Listening to a job interview

5 **Listen to part of a job interview.**

a Which of the jobs in Exercise 4 is the man applying for?

b Listen again and complete the interviewer's notes about the applicant's skills and interests.

```
NOTES
SKILLS: TYPING

INTERESTS: SKIING
```

Grammar: *can / can't*

6 **Look at these extracts from the interview.**
I can speak Spanish.
I can't write business letters in Spanish.
Can you type?

a What form of the verb follows *can*?

b How do we make a question with *can*?

7 **Now look at these sentences.**
Can we leave now? No, you can't.
Can they come tomorrow? He can come, but she can't.
Ms Jones cannot meet you on Tuesday.

a Does the form of *can* change with different subjects (he, she, we, they etc.)?

b Find two negative forms of *can*. Which is for spoken and which is for written English?

▶▶ p.36 **Grammar backup 4**

Vocabulary: skills

8 **Look at the verbs and the nouns below. Match each noun with a verb.**

EXAMPLE: *type letters*

verbs	nouns	
type	the guitar	the piano
use	a bicycle	a horse
speak	letters	a telex machine
play	foreign	poetry
drive	languages	a car
ride	a computer	a bus
write	tennis	a report
	a fax machine	English

Speaking: skills

9 **List your skills, using the phrases in Exercise 8.**

EXAMPLE: *I can play the guitar, but I can't play the piano.*

10 **Work in pairs. Ask your partner about his / her skills. Then tell the class about them.**

Grammar: *like / enjoy + -ing*

11 **What form of the verb follows *like* and *enjoy* in the sentences below?**

What do you like doing in your spare time?
First of all sports. I enjoy skiing …

12 **List five things that you like doing and five things that you do not like doing. Give reasons.**

EXAMPLE: *I like travelling. It's interesting.*

▶▶ p.37 **Grammar backup 4**

Speaking: likes and dislikes

13 **Work in pairs. Ask about your partner's interests.**

EXAMPLE: *What do you enjoy doing?*
I like walking in the country.
Really? Why?
It's relaxing.
What don't you like doing?
I don't enjoy travelling to work every day.

Phrasebook

Likes and dislikes

What do you like doing?
Do you like meeting new people?
Do you enjoy using computers?
I like travelling.
I don't enjoy flying.

Talking point

PEOPLE WORK BETTER WHEN THEY WORK ALONE.

What do *you* think?

Action **B**

The right qualities?

- Describe personal qualities
- Write an advertisement
- Vocabulary:
  - personal qualities
  - adjectives in advertisements

Reading about personal qualities

1 Read these extracts from letters. The writers are applying for jobs. They are explaining why they are good for the job. What kind of job do you think each person is applying for?

A job like this needs a hard-working, well-organised person who is also honest. I think I have these qualities. I also get on well with people at work; I am friendly and try to be helpful.

I think I am right for the job because I am very patient and do not get angry about silly things. People tell me that I am warm and kind. I know I am good with children because I have got younger brothers and sisters.

2 Now look at the situations below. Find an adjective in the letters above to describe each person.

a A man telephones a friend twenty times before the friend answers. The man is not angry. He is patient.

b A child finds a bag with a lot of money in it. She takes it to a police station. She is ..... .

c A stranger at a party is standing alone. You welcome him and start a conversation. You are ..... .

d Your colleague stays at work until 9.00 p.m. to finish a report. She is ..... .

e Someone in your office is having a problem with his computer. You solve the problem. You are ..... .

f The manager cannot find an important letter. Her secretary knows exactly where it is. The secretary is ..... .

3 Find words in the letters that mean the opposite of:

a unfriendly   e lazy
b unhelpful   f impatient
c unkind   g dishonest
d cold   h badly-organised

Vocabulary: personal qualities

4 Look at the adjectives below. Which two usually have a negative meaning? Use a dictionary to help you.

creative	artistic	imaginative	clean	efficient
well-organised	honest	friendly	stubborn	
hard-working	patient	aggressive		

5 Look at the pictures below. Choose three adjectives that describe important qualities for each job. Give reasons.

nurse

sales representative

shop assistant

architect

accountant

receptionist

6 Work in pairs. Tell your partner about some of your personal qualities.

Vocabulary: advertisements

7 Look at advertisements A and B.

a Does the word *sale* tell you that things are:
  • new in the shop?   • good quality?   • cheap?

b Which three other words give you the same information?

c When does the sale begin?

d What do you think the extra adjectives in advertisement B mean? Why are the adjectives there?

8 Look at the adjectives below. Use a dictionary to help you.

fantastic	huge	incredible	great	unbelievable
enormous	wonderful	massive	amazing	giant

a Find four words that mean *very big*.

b Find three words that mean *very (very) nice*.

c Find three words that mean *difficult to believe*.

Writing an advertisement

9 Rewrite this advertisement. Change or add words to make it better.

A

SALE!

Bargains!

Discounts!

Reductions!

• guitars
  • keyboards
    • drums
      • harmonicas
        • books
          • sheet music
            • accessories

STARTS JAN. 1ST

SOUNDS UNLIMITED

High Street, Oxford

B

GIANT SALE!

Fantastic bargains!

Amazing discounts!

Incredible reductions!

• guitars
  • keyboards
    • drums
      • harmonicas
        • books
          • sheet music
            • accessories

STARTS JAN. 1ST

SOUNDS UNLIMITED

High Street, Oxford

Action **C** # The right person?

- Describe personal qualities
- Complete an application form
- Write an accompanying letter
- Ask polite questions
- Take part in a job interview
- Grammar / vocabulary:
  frequency adverbs

Discussion: the right applicant

1 These two people are applying for a job as a secretary. Who do you think is the right person for the job? Why?

EXAMPLE: *I think the man on the left is friendly. He's got a friendly face.*

APPLICATION FORM

Position

Personal details
Surname:
Address:

First name(s):

Fax:
Place of birth:

Telephone:
Date of birth:
Nationality:

Education
Qualificat

Exper
Job

Fernandez de la Hoz 92
28010 Madrid

17th April 1997

Dear Sir/Madam
I enclose my application for the position of ....

Personal qualities I can bring to the position are:
- *I am ....*

I look forward to hearing from you.

Yours faithfully

Writing: applying for a job

2 **Look at the application form and the accompanying letter.**

a Complete the first part of the application form for a job with information about yourself.

b Look at the letter. Choose a job. Why are you a good person for this job? Write a paragraph about your personal qualities.

Speaking and Listening: asking polite questions

3 Imagine you are at an interview for one of the jobs on page 30. What questions do you want to ask?

EXAMPLE: *How much is the salary?*

4  Listen to the end of an interview. Which of these does the job applicant ask about?

salary	lunch breaks	holidays
clothes	working hours	car park

5 When the applicant asks questions, he is very polite. Listen again and complete his questions.

a ..... about the salary first?

b And ..... about holidays too?

c ..... about the working hours?

Ask polite questions about the other points in Exercise 4.

EXAMPLE: *Can I ask about lunch breaks?*

Grammar: frequency adverbs

6 Read the information about the job below. The adverbs (in *italics*) are wrong. Rewrite the sentences with the correct adverbs.

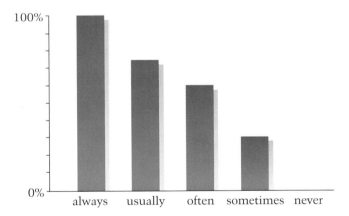

a People *always* take holidays at Christmas, Easter and in the summer.

b The offices are *never* open on Sundays.

c People *usually* work in the evenings.

7 Use adverbs to complete true sentences about yourself.

a I am ..... late for my English class.

b I ..... do my homework.

c I ..... enjoy classes.

d I ..... understand the lesson.

e I ..... take part in activities.

▶▶ p.37 **Grammar backup 4**

Speaking: a job interview

8 Work in pairs.

A: Turn to page 138.

B: You are an applicant for the job in advertisement A. Answer your partner's questions. At the end of the interview, ask about the salary, holidays and working hours.

A

> **Bar staff wanted for busy**
> **night club in luxury hotel**
> **Apply to: Box 133**

Now interview your partner for the job below. Ask about personal details, skills and interests. Answer his / her questions with this information about the job:

Salary: £15,000 a year

Holidays: 3 weeks + public holidays

Hours: 9.00 a.m. – 5.30 p.m.

> **Small, friendly travel agency needs new**
> **staff. No experience necessary.**
> **Apply to: Box 782**

B

Word file   Unit 4

DESCRIBING JOBS
boring
dull
exciting
frightening
fun
interesting
relaxing
stressful
terrifying

PERSONAL QUALITIES
aggressive
artistic
cold

creative
efficient
(un)friendly
hard-working
(un)helpful
(dis)honest
imaginative
(un)kind
lazy
(im)patient
stubborn
warm
well-organised

FREQUENCY
always
never

often
sometimes
usually

'ADVERTISING' ADJECTIVES
amazing
enormous
fantastic
giant
great
huge
incredible
massive
unbelievable

can / can't

Practice

1 Look at the information about two job applicants. Complete the sentences below with *can / can't*.

	Juan	Yvette
type	✓	✓
speak French	✗	✓
speak Spanish	✓	✗
speak English	✓	✓
use a computer	✗	✓
drive	✓	✓
keep accounts	✓	✗
start work now	✓	✗

a Juan and Yvette *can* type.
b Juan ..... speak French but Yvette ..... .
c Yvette ..... use a computer but Juan ..... .
d They ..... both drive.
e Juan ..... start work now but Yvette ..... .
f They ..... speak English.
g ..... Yvette speak Spanish? No, she ..... .
h ..... the two of them keep accounts? No, Juan ..... but Yvette ..... .

2 Make questions for these answers. Use *can*.

a No, I can't. I can't play any musical instruments.
   Can you play a musical instrument?
b My daughter? Yes, she can swim very well.
c Yes. But he's not very good at <u>writing</u> English.
d No, sorry, you can't use the Meeting Room. It's full.
e I don't think I can finish it today, but I can do it tomorrow.
f Yes. The salary is £15,000 a year.

3 Translation

   Write these sentences in your own language.

a I can't understand you.
b Can you type?
c We cannot meet on April 20th.
d She can repair office equipment.
e Can you tell me about the holidays, please?

Reference

An important use of **can** / **can't** is to talk about skills or abilities.

EXAMPLE: I **can** speak a little French.

Can is followed by an infinitive (without *to*).

Statements

I You He She It We They	can can't/cannot	translate.

Can't and **cannot** are both negative forms. We use **cannot** in formal writing. We never use **do** / **does** with **can** to make negative forms or questions.

Questions

Can	I you he/she/it we they	**understand** Italian?

Short answers

Yes,	I you he/she/it we they	can.
No,	I you he/she/it we they	can't.

We also use **can** to ask polite questions and to ask for something.

EXAMPLES: **Can** I ask about holidays?
           Can you tell me about working hours?
           Can I have a cup of coffee, please?

Verb patterns: *like / enjoy + -ing*

Practice

1 Complete this interview extract with a correct form of the verb in brackets.

A: So, can I ask you about your interests? What do you like (a) *doing?* (do)

B: Well, I like (b)..... (travel) and (c)..... (visit) other countries.

A: Ah, you enjoy (d)..... (travel). Do you (e)..... (travel) alone?

B: Sometimes, but I usually (f)..... (go) with a friend.

A: Why don't you enjoy (g)..... (travel) alone?

B: Well, it's no fun. I hate (h)..... (arrive) in a new place on my own. Another interest is sports. I love (i)..... (cycle) and (j)..... (swim) and one or two other sports.

A: Do you like (k)..... (play) tennis?

B: Well, I can play, but I'm not very good.

Frequency adverbs

Practice

1 Rewrite these sentences with the adverbs in the correct place.

a We go to Spain in the summer. (often)
We often go to Spain in the summer.
b I want to see her again. (never)
c It is cold in June in Britain. (sometimes)
d In many countries, trains arrive on time. (always)
e Shops don't close before six o'clock in the evening. (usually)

2 Complete these sentences with the best frequency adverb.

a Vegetarians *never* eat meat.
b You eat in restaurants four evenings a week? So you ..... eat out.
c I don't go out in the evening very much, but I ..... go to see a film.
d It's very important. At the end of the day we ..... take the money to the bank.

3 Write five sentences that are true for you. Use the frequency adverbs in the reference box.

Reference

We use **like**, **dislike**, **hate**, **enjoy** and **love** to talk about activities we like or do not like. These verbs are often followed by the **-ing** form of other verbs.

EXAMPLES: He **enjoys skiing.**
I **love travelling.**
I **don't like being** late.

2 Translation
Write these sentences in your own language.

a I enjoy swimming.
b She doesn't like driving.

Reference

Frequency adverbs answer the question:
How often ...?
EXAMPLE: **How often** do you have lunch at work?

0% **never**
sometimes
often
usually
100% **always**

Frequency adverbs often come before the main verb.
EXAMPLE: We **often** work late.
They come after **be**, **can** and **have**.
EXAMPLE: We are **often** late.
Sometimes can also come at the beginning or end of a sentence.
EXAMPLES: We **sometimes** work late.
Sometimes we work late.
We work late **sometimes**.

5

- Describe a company's business
- Describe the structure of a company
- Vocabulary:
  - support staff
  - work activities
- Grammar:
  - *there is / there are*

In F●cus

Burson-Marsteller is an international public relations company. There are sixty-four Burson-Marsteller offices on five continents. Paul Vosloo is the Managing Director of Burson-Marsteller in Poland and his office is in Warsaw. He and his staff help foreign and Polish companies to increase their business in Poland. Burson-Marsteller gives information and advice, makes introductions and organises events. This helps clients to sell their products and services.

Burson-Marsteller

Reading about a company

1 **Look at the pictures and the text.**
a Find a business card.
b Find a sign outside a building.
c What is Paul Vosloo's job?
d Which company does he work for?
e Which city does he work in?
f Is Burson-Marsteller a small company?
g Does Burson-Marsteller work for other companies?

2 **Find words in the the text to complete the sentences.**
a The boss of Burson-Marsteller in Poland is called the ..... .
b Most of the other ..... are Polish.
c Their ..... are from a number of countries.
d The company gives ..... about public relations.
   Use a dictionary to check other new words.

B Burson-Marsteller
Public Relations

Paul Vosloo
Managing Director

Burson-Marsteller

Public Relations/Public Affairs

IMM Centre
ul. Krzywickiego 34/B
02-078 Warszawa
Telephone: (88 2) 625 55 30, 625 53 96
Facsimile: (48 2) 625 55 41
Int'l Tel/Fax: (48) 39123237

Writing: describing a company's business

3 **Look at these verbs and the company logos. Use the verbs to write about the companies.**
   EXAMPLE: *Coca-Cola makes drinks.*

   make   sell   publish   lend   fly

Listening: the structure of a company

4 🎧 **Listen. One of the staff at Burson-Marsteller is describing the different jobs in the company. Match the jobs with the boxes.**

General Manager   support staff
Account Executives   Group Directors
Deputy General Manager   Account Managers

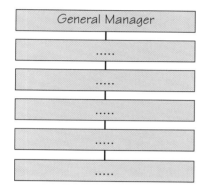

Vocabulary: support staff

5 **Match the jobs of the support staff with the pictures.**

receptionist   technician   security guard
cleaner   telephonist   clerk

6 **Write about the jobs in Exercise 5. Use verbs and nouns from the lists below.**

EXAMPLE: *A telephonist answers the telephone.*

VERBS		NOUNS	
answer	welcome	equipment	the doors
guard	help	documents	the floors
sweep	clean	visitors	the telephone
lock	file	the offices	machines
repair		the building	

Listening and Reading: describing the structure of a company

7 🎧 **Listen and read. What are the missing words?**

I'm a receptionist. There are two of us on the front desk. Above me (a)..... ..... an Office Manager. He's also responsible for all the secretaries. (b)..... ..... about six secretaries. Then (c)..... ..... the Administration Manager. She's one of four managers, and above them is the Director.

Grammar: *there is / there are*

8 **There are grammar mistakes in three of the sentences below. Find them and correct them.**

a There's six secretaries in the company.
b Are there any male secretaries?
c There is a security guard here.
d There are some visitors at reception.
e There is some clients in the meeting room.
f There isn't a computer at reception.
g Are there any coffee?

▶▶ p.44 **Grammar backup 5**

Speaking: describing the structure of a company

9 **Work in pairs. Describe a company or organisation that you know. Use expressions from the Phrasebook.**

Phrasebook

Describing company structure

There are ten **of us.**
There is an Administration Manager.
Above her **there's** an Office Manager.
Below her **there are** two other managers.
Our boss is an Englishman.
He's responsible for the secretaries.

Action B Finding the way

- Describe location
- Give directions
- Vocabulary:
  - companies and organisations
  - short forms
  - ordinal numbers
- Grammar:
  prepositions of place

Vocabulary: companies and organisations

1 Look at the picture below.
Where are these people?
What is the woman's job?

LANGDALE BUSINESS CENTRE

Floor	Company
11th	National Oil Co.
10th	European School of Business
9th	M.I.T. Insurance
8th	Media Mix
7th	Bacano Drinks Ltd.
6th	Blake Property Inc.
5th	Bank of Europe
4th	Challenge Security
3rd	Dept. of Agriculture
2nd	Langdale Publishing
1st	Bailey International
Ground	Enquiries
Basement	Restaurant
	Cafeteria
	WC

2 Look at the sign for the Langdale Business Centre. Which company or organisation:

a prints and sells books?
b buys and sells buildings?
c provides staff to guard buildings?
d makes television programmes?
e lends money?
f is a government department?
Use a dictionary to help you.

3 Which short form means:

a department? *dept.*   d company?
b toilet?   e limited?
c incorporated?   f first?

Listening to numbers

4 Listen. Say the name of the company or organisation.
EXAMPLE: *Cassette: 'It's on the first floor.'*
You: 'Bailey International.'

Vocabulary: ordinal numbers

5 Look at the ordinal numbers on the left. Write the short form of each number.

6 Listen and repeat the numbers in order.

7 Work in pairs. Look at the sign for the Langdale Business Centre again. Ask and answer about the companies on the sign.
EXAMPLE: *Excuse me. Where's the Bank of Europe?*
It's on the fifth floor, sir / madam.

a	first lst	g	fourth
b	eleventh	h	third
c	fifth	i	sixth
d	tenth	j	ninth
e	twelfth	k	seventh
f	eighth	l	second

Listening and Speaking: describing location

8 Look at this plan. Is the information true or false?

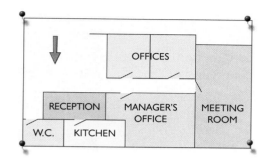

a The kitchen is near the meeting room.
b The manager's office is along the corridor, on the left.
c The meeting room is at the end of the corridor.
d The reception desk is opposite the main entrance.

9 🔊 **Listen and find these buildings on the map below.**

- Ministry of Information *C*
- Inter-fashion
- Jet Travel
- Euro Exports
- Pan Music
- Britinvest
- National Metals

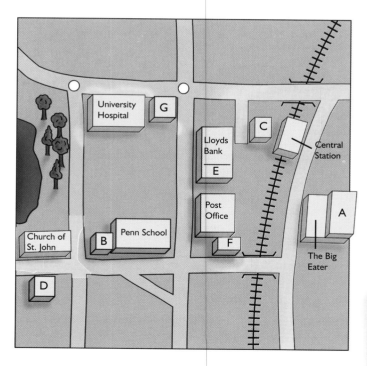

10 Work in pairs. Ask and answer about the location of these companies.

  EXAMPLE: *Where's the Ministry of Information?*
  It's near / behind the station.

Listening and Reading: giving directions

11 🔊 **A receptionist is giving directions to Burson-Marsteller. Listen and read. Find the company's location on the map below.**

> *Visitor:* How do I get to the office? I've got a map here.
> *Receptionist:* Can you find the Marriott Hotel?
> *Visitor:* The Marriott Hotel ... Yes, here it is.
> *Receptionist:* OK. You turn left out of the hotel and left again. Then go straight on and you take the third street on the right.
> *Visitor:* Third on the right ...
> *Receptionist:* Yes, and we're in the first street on the left, on the left-hand side.
> *Visitor:* Ah, yes. Thank you.

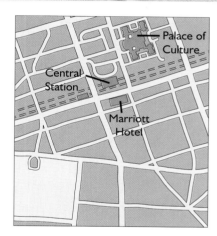

▶▶ p.45 **Grammar backup 6**

Speaking: giving directions

12 Work in pairs. Use expressions from the Phrasebook.

  A: Think of a well-known place in the town / city where you are now. Ask your partner where the place is and how to get there.

  B: Give your partner the information he / she needs.

Phrasebook

Asking for and giving directions

Where's the bus station?
How do I get to the office?
Is this the way to the coffee bar?
Turn right.
Turn left.
Go straight on.
Take the next road **on the** left.

Action | C

First impressions

- Make polite offers and requests
- Welcome visitors
- Vocabulary:
    personal qualities

Vocabulary: personal qualities

1 Look at the pictures.

a Which company has a good receptionist?

b Which receptionist or reception desk do these adjectives describe?
Use a dictionary to help you.

| friendly | untidy | unattractive | professional | helpful |
| unfriendly | tidy | attractive | unprofessional | unhelpful |

Listening and Speaking: polite offers and requests

2 🔊 Listen and read. Which sentences are friendly and polite?

a • What do you want?
  • Can I help you?

b • Fill in the visitor's book.
  • Can you fill in the visitor's book, please?

c • Can I have your name?
  • Name?

d • Sit down for a moment.
  • Would you take a seat for a moment?

Do you use similar expressions in your language when you want to be polite?

3 Change these sentences. Make them friendly and polite. Use expressions from the Phrasebook.

a Give me your coat.

b Spell your surname.

c Write your name here.

d I want a drink.

Phrasebook

Polite offers and requests

Can I help you?
Can you sign here, **please?**
Would you take a seat?
I'd like a taxi, **please.**

4 🔊 **A receptionist is talking to a visitor. Listen and answer these questions.**

a Who does the visitor want to see?
b What time is his appointment?
c What is the visitor's name?
d Who does he work for?

5 🔊 **Listen to the conversation again, and fill in the visitor's book for the visitor.**

Name	Company	Visiting	Time in	Time out
John Steel	Brand Plastics	Mr Janiurek	2.15	

Speaking: welcoming a visitor at reception

6 **Work in pairs.**

A: Turn to page 138.
B: You are a receptionist. Welcome your visitor and announce his / her arrival. Then take the role of the visitor. Use the information below.

Thursday   APRIL 7

10.00 a.m. Ms Fletcher, Bank of Europe

Martin Paper Ltd
Peter J Dalton
Marketing Manager

Listening to telephone conversations

7 🔊 **Listen to three conversations at reception. Which of these items does the receptionist need for each conversation?**

8 🔊 **Listen to one of the conversations again and correct the message.**

MESSAGE
To: Mrs Smith
From: Mr Allouit
Message: He is not free this afternoon. Can he meet you for lunch at 12.30 next Tuesday? Please phone him.

Talking point

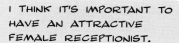
I THINK IT'S IMPORTANT TO HAVE AN ATTRACTIVE FEMALE RECEPTIONIST.

What do *you* think?

Word file   Unit 5

JOBS
cleaner
clerk
director
receptionist
secretary
security guard
support staff
technician
telephonist

PERSONAL QUALITIES
(un)attractive
(un)professional
(un)tidy

ORDINAL NUMBERS
first
second
third
fourth
fifth
sixth
seventh
eighth
ninth
tenth
eleventh

VERBS
answer
design
file
fly

guard
hear
help
lend
publish
see
sweep

OTHER
basement
cafeteria
client
event
floor
information
public relations
responsible for
restaurant
WC / toilet

there is / there are

Practice

1 Complete these sentences with *there is(n't)* or *there are(n't)*.

a There is a good restaurant next door.
b ..... any trains this evening.
c ..... three people in reception.
d ..... some water on the table.
e ..... some glasses on the shelf.
f ..... any meetings on Saturday.
g ..... some customers at the door.
h ..... any money in the till.
i ..... no tea in the kitchen.

2 Look at the picture. Complete the questions and give short answers.

a Is there a counter near the main door?
  Yes there is.
b ..... a desk behind the counter? ..... .
c ..... any small tables near the counter? ..... .
d ..... a fax machine on the desk? ..... .
e ..... a computer on the desk? ..... .
f ..... three people in the picture? ..... .
g ..... any flowers on the counter? ..... .

3 Which <u>underlined</u> words have short forms?

a <u>There is</u> a new assistant today.
  <u>Is there</u>?
b <u>There are</u> mistakes in this letter.
  <u>There are not</u>!

Reference

We use **there is** or **there are** to give new information about something that exists or something that is · present.

Statements

We use **there is (not)** with singular or uncountable nouns.

EXAMPLES: ***There's*** *a visitor.*
           There isn't *any coffee.*

We use **there are (not)** with plural nouns.

EXAMPLE: ***There are*** *hundreds of new companies in Poland.*

Questions
Is there ...?
Are there ...?

Short answers

Yes,	there is/there are.
No,	there isn't/there is not. there aren't/there are not.

Short forms

there is = **there's**
(We do not use this short form in short answers.)
there is not = **there isn't**
there are not = **there aren't**

4 Translation
  Write these sentences in your own language.

a There's a receipt on your desk.
b Is there any coffee?
c Are there any messages?
d There aren't any British managers.

Prepositions of place

Practice

1 Complete these sentences with *on* or *in*.

a It's the second door *on* the right.
b The offices are ..... a large building opposite the station.
c The meeting is ..... the second floor.
d It's ..... meeting room A.
e The cafeteria's ..... the basement.

2 Look at the map. Complete these directions.

You ..... out of this building and ..... left. ..... the second road on the left and the hotel's just around the corner.

Which building is the hotel?

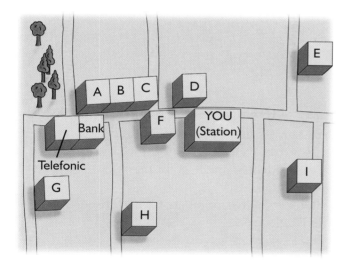

Reference

Prepositions of place answer the question **Where ...?**

It's	on the (first) floor. on the right/left. in the building. in that room. in the basement. in Oxford Street.

It's	behind near next door to above opposite round the corner from in the same street as	the hotel.

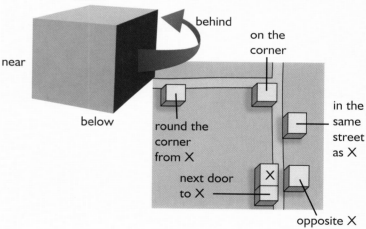

3 Look at the map again and complete these directions.

Our office is ..... as the station. You turn left out of the station, walk about a hundred metres and Telefonic Ltd is ..... the park, ... the bank.

4 Translation

Write these sentences in your own language.

a You turn left near the cinema.
b The office is on the ground floor, behind the main reception desk.
c You take the second on the right.
d It's next door to a restaurant.

... AND IT'S OPPOSITE THE BANK.

Contacts

6

Action **A** ■ Take and leave telephone messages
■ Grammar:
    past simple (regular verbs)

Telephone messages

Listening to telephone messages

1 🔊 **Listen to three extracts from telephone conversations.**

a Match them with the messages below.
b Which caller is speaking to a machine?

A

FOR: PAUL VOSLOO   FROM: DAVID MCQUID

OF: ING BANK   DATE: **31/1**
                                                 TIME: **12.20** p.m.

TEL: FAX: TAKEN BY: **M. S.**
    CODE   NUMBER EXT.   CODE   NUMBER

TELEPHONED ○ PLEASE RING BACK ✗ RETURNED YOUR CALL ○ WILL RING BACK ○ WOULD LIKE TO SEE YOU ○ URGENT ✗

B
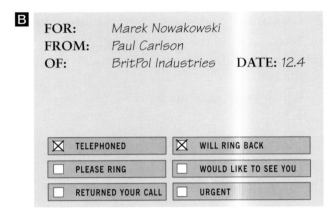

FOR:	Marek Nowakowski	
FROM:	Paul Carlson	
OF:	BritPol Industries	DATE: 12.4

☒ TELEPHONED	☒ WILL RING BACK
☐ PLEASE RING	☐ WOULD LIKE TO SEE YOU
☐ RETURNED YOUR CALL	☐ URGENT

C

MESSAGE

To: Hanna Dymek
From: Jennifer Simons
Message:

Please call her after 3.00 tomorrow.

2 🔊 **Listen to another conversation and choose the correct answers.**

a Magda Kranz called: • in the morning. • at four o'clock.
    • in the afternoon. • at two o'clock.
b She phoned about: • an advertisement. • an interview.
    • a job. • an appointment.
c She needed to speak to: • the receptionist. • Mr Hanson.
    • a secretary. • Mrs Hughes.
d She wanted to: • phone again. • leave a message.
    • speak to another person. • write a letter.

Grammar: past simple (regular verbs)

3 **Look at the conversation below.**

a Find verbs that refer to the past. How are they formed?

> *Mrs Hughes:* Did Mrs Kranz call again?
> *Receptionist:* Yes, she phoned yesterday evening. I tried your extension, but your secretary didn't answer.
> *Mrs Hughes:* No, she stopped work at five, her son's ill. If Mrs Kranz calls again, ask her to write to me, please.

b Write the past simple forms of these verbs.

    live   cry   shop

4 Complete these charts with the past simple of the verb *call*.

Statements

I You He She We They	.... not	last week. this morning. yesterday. from Germany. about a job.

Questions

Why When Who	.....	I you he she we they	..... ?

 p.52   **Grammar backup 6**

Listening: telephone talk

5  Listen again to the beginning of the conversation between Magda Kranz and the receptionist. Write the words that the speakers use to:

a answer the telephone.
b ask for someone.
c connect someone.
d thank someone.

6 **Which of these expressions does a caller use? Which expressions does a receptionist use?**

a Would you like to leave a message?
b Can I take a message?
c Can I leave a message?
d Can I give her a message?
e Could you give him a message?

Speaking and Listening: taking and leaving messages

7 **Work in pairs. Use expressions from the Phrasebook.**

A: You are a receptionist or a secretary. Answer the telephone and take a message.

B: Call your partner, using your name and the name of your company or a company in your town. Choose one of the situations below and leave a message for the boss, Mr Adams.

• You are ill and can't go to a meeting.
• You want to leave your fax number.
• Your plane arrives at six o'clock.

Then change roles.

8 Listen and read. Answer these questions about the answerphone message below.

a When can you ring again?
b What information do you include in your message?
c When do you speak?

> THANK YOU FOR CALLING PNT. WE ARE OPEN FIVE DAYS A WEEK BETWEEN 9.00 A.M. AND 6.00 P.M. PLEASE CALL AGAIN, OR LEAVE YOUR NAME, NUMBER AND MESSAGE AFTER THE TONE.

9 Work in pairs.

A: You have a new answerphone. Write your own recorded message. Read it to your partner.

B: Leave a message on A's answerphone. Start like this:
Hello. This is (your name) at (the time) on (the day).

Then change roles.

Phrasebook

Answering the telephone

Burson-Marsteller. **Can I help you?**
Susan Cooper **speaking.**
Good morning. Sales department.

Asking for someone

Can I speak to Mr Holden, **please?**
Could I speak to the manager?
I'd like to speak to Jane Speed.
Is Peter Phillips **there, please?**

Action B

Connections

- Deal with callers
- Make excuses
- Deal with correspondence
- Vocabulary:
  - types of telephone
  - telephone language

Vocabulary: types of telephone

1 Match the pictures A – F with words from the list below.

a mobile phone	a videophone	an answerphone
a switchboard	a fax machine	a pay phone

2 Which telephone(s) can you use to:

a call from a station?   d send a written message?

b call from your car?   e connect a caller to another phone?

c record a message?   f see the caller?

Listening to telephone conversations

3 Listen and complete the conversations.

a

Receptionist: Tall Orders. Can I help you?

Caller: Good morning. ..... speak to John Penright, please?

Receptionist: Just a moment, I'll ..... to his secretary.

b

Secretary: Mr Penright's office. Gary ..... .

Caller: Good morning. ..... Tony Bates of Cagny Distribution. I'd like a word with Mr Penright about our new contract. Is Mr Penright .....?

Secretary: Yes, he is. ..... put you through.

Vocabulary: telephone language

4 Look at these sentences. For each <u>underlined</u> part, find words or phrases in the list below with a similar meaning.

a I'd like to <u>speak to</u> the manager, please. talk to .....

b Could he <u>phone</u> you later? ....

c I'll <u>put</u> you <u>through</u> now. .....

d She's <u>in</u> this afternoon. ....

connect	in the office	call	talk to
here	have a word with	ring	

Listening and Speaking: dealing with callers

5 Listen. Complete the receptionist's responses and practise saying them.

a I'm afraid he isn't here at the moment.

b Yes, but ..... .

c Yes, ...

d I'm not sure. ..... .

e Certainly. I'll ..... .

f I'm sorry, ...

Speaking: making excuses

6 Look at the pictures. Which of the explanations describes each situation.

I'm afraid		not in the office.
		ill.
	she's	on the telephone.
I'm sorry		in a meeting.
		on holiday / away.
		at lunch.

Speaking: answering the telephone

7 Work in pairs.

A: Turn to page 138.

B: You are the receptionist at Sport Ace, a company that makes sports equipment. Answer the telephone and try to put the caller through. Then answer the telephone again, and explain why the manager cannot take the call.

Reading: dealing with correspondence

8 Look at the pieces of correspondence below.

a Which did a secretary write?
b Which letter can a secretary open?
c Which messages ask for action today?

A

FOR: PAUL VOSLOO   FROM: DAVID MCQUID
OF: ING BANK
TEL: DATE: 31/1
                        TIME: 12.20P.M.
     CODE NUMBER EXT. FAX: TAKEN BY: M.S.
                        CODE NUMBER

TELEPHONED ○ PLEASE RING BACK ✗ RETURNED YOUR CALL ○ WILL RING BACK ○ WOULD LIKE TO SEE YOU ○ URGENT ✗

B Confidential

Aleksandra Olek
Burson-Marsteller
IMM Centre
ul. Krzywickiego 34/B
02-078 Warszawa

C NO CALLS THIS MORNING THANKS P.V.

D Personal

Mr P. Vosloo
Burson-Marsteller
IMM Centre
ul. Krzywickiego 34/B
02-078 Warsaw
Poland

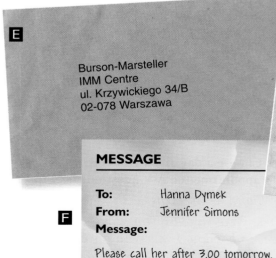

E

Burson-Marsteller
IMM Centre
ul. Krzywickiego 34/B
02-078 Warszawa

MESSAGE

F

To: Hanna Dymek
From: Jennifer Simons
Message:

Please call her after 3.00 tomorrow.

Action **C** Appointments

- Make appointments
- Apologise and make excuses
- Grammar:
  was / were

Reading a diary

1 Susan Reilly is a company director. Look at her computer diary.

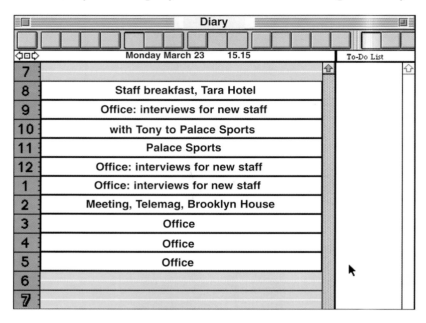

Give short answers to these questions.

a What is the date?
b What day is it?
c Where is Susan now?
d Where was Susan at eight o'clock?
e Who was she with?
f Where were Susan and Tony at eleven o'clock?
g When was she free to answer the phone?

Grammar: was / were

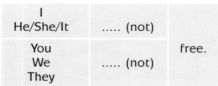

I He/She/It	..... (not)	
You We They	..... (not)	free.

2 Complete the chart on the left with the past forms of the verb *to be*.

3 Complete the text below with *was, was not, were* or *were not*.

At eight o'clock, Susan and her staff ..... in the office. They ..... at a local hotel. From 10 o'clock, Susan ..... at Palace Sports with Tony for a couple of hours. She ..... in her office between twelve and two, but she ..... free to answer the phone.

⟩⟩ p.53 Grammar backup 6

4 Work in pairs. Choose a day and a time last week. Ask your partner about his / her appointments. Ask questions beginning with:

Where ... ?   *Who ... with?*   *Why ... ?*

EXAMPLE: *Where were you last Thursday?*
         I was in London. I was with my colleague.

Then tell another person in the class about your partner.

Speaking: making appointments

5 🔊 **Listen and read. How do you think this phone conversation continues?**

> *Secretary:* Reilly Associates. Good afternoon.
> *Caller:* Oh, hello. This is Marc Bedouelle. Could I speak to Mrs Reilly, please?
> *Secretary:* I'm afraid she's in a meeting, Mr Bedouelle.
> *Caller:* Well, can I make an appointment for Mr Clerc to see her later this afternoon? Is she free at half past three?
> *Secretary:* .....

Listen to the whole conversation and check your answer.

6 **Work in pairs.**

A: Turn to page 138.
B: Mrs Reilly is your boss and you have her diary. Write some appointments in the diary. Leave some spaces. Telephone Mr Ellison and make an appointment for her to see him.

Sunday	15	Thursday	19
Monday	16	Friday	20
Tuesday	17	Saturday	21
Wednesday	18	Notes	

Listening and Speaking: apologising and making excuses

7 🔊 **Listen to the answerphone and make notes. Then write the message.**

MESSAGE

Message for: _____ From: _____
Phone no: _____

8 **Work in the same pairs as for Exercise 6.**

A: You are Mr Ellison's secretary. Answer the telephone and respond to the caller.
B: You are Mrs Reilly's secretary. Telephone Mr Ellison's secretary and try to change Mrs Reilly's appointment. Give a reason for the change. Use expressions from the Phrasebook.

Phrasebook

Apologising

I'm sorry, the office is closed.
I'm very sorry, he isn't here.
I'm so sorry, she can't come.
I'm terribly sorry, he's out today.
I'm afraid he's in a meeting.

Talking point

IT'S EASY TALKING TO AN ANSWERPHONE. TALKING TO PEOPLE IS THE PROBLEM.

What do *you* think?

Word file   Unit 6

ON THE TELEPHONE		OTHER
answerphone	ring	busy
ask for	switchboard	free
caller	tone	out
connect	videophone	sorry
extension	**MESSAGES**	**OTHER**
have a word (with)	confidential	appointment
mobile phone	personal	personnel
pay phone	urgent	manager
recorded message	**EXCUSES**	
	afraid	
	away	

Grammar *backup 6*

Past simple (regular verbs)

Practice

1 Write sentences about yourself at eight years old. Use the phrases in brackets.

a I ..... (play football)
   I didn't play football.
b I ..... (play the piano)
c I ..... (like school)
d I ..... (answer the telephone)
e I ..... (live in a flat)

2 Change these questions and answers to refer to the past.

a What do you play? I play the guitar.
   What did you play? I played the guitar.
b Do you play tennis?
   Yes, I do.
c Where do they live?
   They live in the centre of town.
d Why does she work in a sports shop?
   Because she likes the job.
e Does he walk to work?
   No, he doesn't.

3 Use the past forms of these verbs to complete the story.

> look   shout   move   stop   arrive
> wait   press (x 2)

Tim (a) *arrived* at a hotel late one night. He (b).....
the button in the lift and the lift (c)..... a little.
Then it (d)..... . He (e)....., then he (f)..... the
emergency button, and then he (g)..... for help.
After ten minutes, he (h)..... behind him. There
was a second door there and it was open!

4 Translation
Write these sentences in your own language.

a Did Mrs Brown telephone yesterday?
b I didn't thank him for the flowers.
c I wanted to ask a question.

Reference

We use the past simple to talk about actions, situations and events at a specific time or in a specific period in the past.

The past simple is formed with:

-ed play → play**ed**
-d   like → like**d**
-ied study → stud**ied**
double consonant + **-ed**   stop → stop**ped**

To form questions and negatives we use **did** and the infinitive of the verb.

Statements

I You He She It We They	waited.
	didn't/did not wait.

Questions

Did	I you he she it we they	wait?

Short answers

Yes,	I you he she it we they	did.
No,		didn't/did not.

Past simple: *to be*

Practice

1 Write short answers about yourself as a child.

a Were you good at schoolwork?
No, I wasn't.

b Were you good at sports?

c Were your teachers kind to you?

d Was your father a good cook?

e Was your mother at home all day?

f Were you the only child?

2 Look at the table below and complete the text with *was(n't)* or *were(n't)*.

telephone	✓
answerphone	✗
mobile phone	✗
fax machine	✓
e-mail	✗

When I was a child, there (a) *was* a telephone in the house, but there (b)..... an answerphone and there (c)..... any mobile phones. There (d)..... fax machines in those days, but there (e)..... any e-mail.

3 You met a woman at an office party last night. Your friend is asking about her. Write your friend's questions and your answers.

a client?
Was she a new client?
Yes, she was.

b What / name?

c Where / from?

d What / job?

e Why / at the party?

New client:
Angeles Rodriguez (Mrs)
Company: Total Plastics, Chile
Position: General Manager
Reason for visit: to meet staff

4 Translation

Write these sentences in your own language.

a Were you in the office yesterday?

b My boss was at a meeting in the afternoon.

c We weren't busy before lunch.

Reference

The past simple forms of the verb **to be** are **was** and **were**.

Statements

I He She It	was	there.
	wasn't/was not	
You We They	were	
	weren't/were not	

Questions

Was	I? he? she? it?
Were	you? we? they?

Short answers

Yes,	I/he/she/it	was.
	you/we/they	were.
No,	I/he/she/it	wasn't. was not.
	you/we/they	weren't. were not.

WHAT WERE YOU INTERESTED IN AS A CHILD?

I WAS ALWAYS INTERESTED IN BUSINESS.

Action A

Planning a business trip

- Understand travel arrangements
- Arrange a meeting
- Vocabulary:
  - months of the year
  - dates
- Grammar:
  have got to

Discussion: making travel arrangements

1 **Your boss asks you to make all the travel arrangements for his / her business trip.**
a What information do you need from your boss?
b Which people and companies do you contact to make the arrangements for the trip?

Listening: preparing for a business trip

2 🔊 **Listen. Your boss is telling you about the business trip.**
a Complete the notes on the left.
b Which company is she visiting on the trip?
c Which of these jobs does your boss want you to do?

- book flights
- book hotels
- book a taxi
- arrange meetings
- write letters to companies abroad

```
DEPARTURE DATE: _____
RETURN TO WARSAW: _____

PLACE          NUMBER OF DAYS
LONDON              3
.....               2
BARCELONA          .....
FRANKFURT          .....
.....               4
```

Grammar: *have got to*

3 **Look at these sentences from Exercise 2.**

*I leave Warsaw on April 2nd and **I've got to** be back in the office on April 18th.*
***I've got to** visit the Barcelona office.*

a Is there a problem if she gets back to her office on April 19th?
b Is it important that she visits the Barcelona office?
c Begin the sentences with *she*. How do the verb forms change?
d Complete this question:
'When ..... she ..... be back in the office?'
'On April 18th.'

Talking point

TRAVEL IS A LEARNING EXPERIENCE.

What do *you* think?

4 **Complete these sentences with the correct forms of *have got to*.**

a I / catch a plane at 9.30 a.m.
I've got to catch a plane at 9.30 a.m.

b you / take any papers?

c the secretary / book hotels?

d the hotel / be in a quiet place.

e when / the boss / be back?

f what time / the boss / be at the airport?

g other people / do her work when she is away.

h she / not / do anything important before she leaves Warsaw.

5 **Work in pairs. Tell your partner what you have got to do before you go to bed tonight.**

EXAMPLE: *I've got to go shopping.*

 p.60 **Grammar backup 7**

Listening: arranging a meeting

6 🔊 **A secretary in Warsaw is speaking to a secretary in London. They are arranging a meeting. Listen and choose the best ending for each sentence.**

a The secretary in London is:
- Jackie.
- Jenny.
- Julie.

b The two secretaries:
- are strangers.
- often speak on the telephone.
- are close friends.

c Ms Pawlowska wants to meet:
- Ms Elliott.
- Mr Arnold.
- Mr Elliott.

d They arrange the meeting for:
- 10.00 a.m. on Tuesday April 9th.
- 10.30 a.m. on Tuesday April 10th.
- 10.30 a.m. on Tuesday April 11th.

e The meeting is:
- for one hour.
- for two hours.
- all morning.

Months of the year	
January	July
February	August
March	September
April	October
May	November
June	December

Vocabulary: dates

7 **Look at the months of the year in English.**

a Which ones are similar in your language?

b How do we say these numbers? • 1st • 2nd • 3rd

c Look at these dates.

January 22nd	March 10th	May 13th
23rd August	1st October	31st July

We write *June 7th* or *7th June*, but we say *June the seventh* or *the seventh of June*. Practise saying the dates above.

Speaking: arranging a meeting

8 **Work in pairs and arrange a meeting. Use expressions from the Phrasebook.**

A: Turn to page 139.

B: You are Ms Pawlowska's secretary. Look at her diary. Telephone Mr Shaw's secretary in London to arrange a meeting. You know the secretary well.

APRIL

Monday 11
2 – 5 p.m. Marketing meeting. Rm 210

Tuesday 12
10.30 – 11.30 Mr Elliott
Lunch – Peter Vincent

Wednesday 13
9 a.m. – 1 p.m. Finance meeting
7 p.m. airport

Phrasebook

Arranging a meeting

I'm phoning to arrange a meeting.
She'd like to see Mr Elliott.
Is he free on Monday?
How about 3 o'clock?
Nice to speak to you.

Hotels

- Understand travel documents
- Vocabulary:
  - hotel rooms
  - hotel facilities
  - types of payment

Vocabulary: hotel rooms

1 Look at this list of prices for rooms in an international hotel. Which types of room do the pictures show?

Suite $350

◆

Double room or twin room

with bath $220

with shower $200

◆

Single room

with bath $150

with shower $140

A
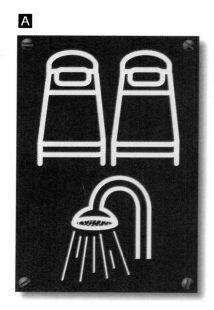

B
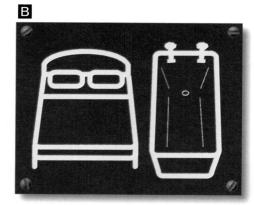

C

D
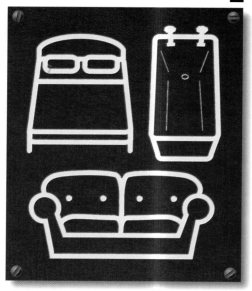

Vocabulary: hotel facilities

2 Look at these hotel facilities. Find words to answer the questions below. Use a dictionary to help you.

bar	restaurant	night club	sports club	swimming pool
squash court	tennis court	business centre	laundry service
satellite TV	travel agency	minibar	room service

a Where can you get some exercise?
b Where can you get a drink?
c Where can you have a meal?
d How can you order food in your room?
e Where can you send a fax?
f Who do you call when your clothes are dirty?
g How can you watch international television programmes?
h Where can you buy a plane ticket?

3 **Put these activities in the order they usually happen.**

A pay

B Following our telephone conversation this morning, I'm writing to ... confirm

C reserve

D leave

E arrive

Reading travel documents

4 **Look at the form and the pictures below.**

a Match each picture with a type of payment.

b Who pays the bill if your company has a *company account*?

Personal details

Name: _____

Address: _____

Passport number: _____

Company _____

Payment details

Cash ☐   Traveller's cheque ☐

Cheque ☐   Company account ☐

Credit card ☐

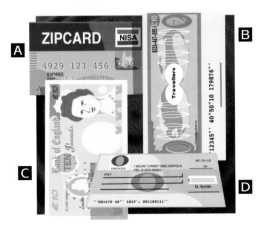

5 **Look at the documents below.**

a Find these words in the documents. What are they in your language?

| bill | receipt | discount | tip | service charge |

b Use the words to complete these sentences.
   • At the bar sandwiches cost $3.50, but in your room you pay a 10% ..... .
   • You have to pay your ..... before you leave a hotel.
   • One bottle of wine costs £5.00. If you buy six bottles there is a 10% ..... , so you pay £27.00.
   • A ..... is the money you give for good service.
   • When you pay your bill, you receive a ..... . This shows how much you paid.

A

Grand Hotel BILL

Mr G. Seal	Room 147
2/4/97	
Room	120.00
Discount 10%	12.00
To pay	108.00

B

RECEIPT FOR HIRING

JOURNEY: PICCADILLY TO PADDINGTON STATION

DATE: APRIL 2ND 1997

SIGNATURE: D. T. JONES   FARE: £5.25

Thank you!

C

HOTEL ESMERELDA

LONDON

ROOM SERVICE MENU

Please note that there is a 10% service charge on all items served in your room.

SANDWICHES .... Chicken £3.50

Giving Tips in Britain

D It is usual to give a 10% tip to taxi-drivers and waiters. If a hotel porter helps you with your bags, £1.00 is a good tip.

Discussion: tips

6 **Look at D again. What do you think about giving tips? Who do you give them to? What is a good tip in your country?**

Action **C**

Booking a room

- Book a hotel room
- Confirm a booking
- Grammar:
  present continuous for the
  future

Discussion: preparing to book a hotel room

1 Before you book a hotel room for your boss, what information do you need? Make a list of questions that hotel receptionists ask.

Listening: booking a hotel room

2 Listen to the telephone conversation.

a Are the receptionist's questions the same as the ones you wrote in Exercise 1?

b Complete the notes on the left, about the booking.

c What has the secretary got to do now?

Name of guest:

Company:

Date of arrival:

Date of departure:

Type of room:

Discount: %

Room rate:

Grammar: present continuous for the future

3 Look at this sentence from the conversation and answer the questions.

He's arriving on the 23rd and leaving on the 24th.

a Is he arriving now or in the future?

b Is he leaving now or in the future?

c Are his plans fixed?

4 Make sentences about the future using the present continuous.

a he / arrive / 6 o'clock.

   He's arriving at 6 o'clock.

b they / finish the meeting in an hour's time.

c we / go to the party next week?

d you / come to the meeting tomorrow?

e you / go on holiday the week after Christmas?

f the company / close soon.

g the new secretary / start the day after tomorrow.

h she / go to South America next month?

5 Each sentence below is a response to a question or statement in Exercise 4. Which one?

1 But I need someone to type the letter today! *g*

2 Is he coming alone?

3 Well, can you give Bill this message when he comes out?

4 Tomorrow! I thought it was the day after!

5 No, the week before.

6 Yes, to Argentina and Brazil, I think.

7 So have you got another job?

8 I'd like to go. What about you?

▶▶ p.61 Grammar backup 7

Phrasebook

Discussing arrangements

Is she coming here soon?
Yes, she's coming next week.
Are you meeting the clients tomorrow?
No, the day after tomorrow.
When are they leaving?
In a week's time.

Speaking: booking a hotel room

6 Work in pairs.

A: Turn to page 139.

B: You are the receptionist at the Royal Hotel. Answer the telephone and take a booking from your partner. Ask questions to complete the form. Then change roles.

Name of guest:

Company:

Date of arrival:

Date of departure:

Type of room:

Discount: %

Room rate:

Reading: confirming a booking

7 Look at the fax on the right that confirms Mr Swallow's booking at the Royal Hotel.

a Does Anna Kowalska work for Berber, the Royal Hotel or Burson-Marsteller?

b Look at these expressions. Find expressions in the fax that they can replace.
  • Following ...
  • I would like to book ...
  • I would be grateful ...
  • ... as soon as possible.

Writing a fax

8 Write a fax confirming the booking in Exercise 6.

Burson-Marsteller

ul. Krzywickiego 34/B
02-078 Warszawa
Telephone: (88 2) 625 55 30, 625 53 96
Facsimile: (48 2) 625 55 41
Int'l Tel/Fax: (48) 39123237

FAX TRANSMISSION

Date: 22.08.1994
To: Ms Hartmann
               Royal Hotel
Fax No: 49–69–69752419
From: Anna Kowalska
Pages: 1
Re: Reservation

With reference to my telephone call today, I would like to reserve a single room with a bath for Mr Swallow from Berber, from 9 p.m. 23.08.94 to 24.08.94

I would appreciate it if you could confirm the reservation by fax a.s.a.p. The payment will be made by Jim Swallow himself.

My telephone number in Poland: 48-2-625-55-30
fax: 48-2-625-55-41

Best regards

Anna Kowalska

Barcelona • Berlin • Brussels • Budapest • Frankfurt • Geneva • The Hague • Hamburg • London • Madrid • Milan • Moscow • Munich • Oslo • Paris • Prague • Rome • Seville • Stockholm • Warsaw • Zurich
Also wholly owned offices throughout Asia • Australia • North America • South America

---

Word file Unit 7

TRAVEL	HOTELS	tennis court
arrange	bar	twin room
arrangement	bath	
arrival	business centre	**PAYMENT**
arrive	double room	account
book	guest	bill
booking	laundry service	discount
confirm	minibar	pay
contact	room service	receipt
depart	satellite TV	service charge
departure	shower	tip
flight	single room	traveller's cheque
reserve	sports club	
return	squash court	**OTHER**
trip	suite	boss
	swimming pool	stranger
		waiter

Grammar *backup 7*

have got to

Practice

1 Complete these sentences with forms of *have got to*.

a I / go to the bank.
  I've got to go to the bank.

b she / be at a meeting.

c when / he / catch his plane?

d how much / we / pay?

e they / not / come on Saturday.

f they / leave now?

g the company / buy new computers.

2 Write sentences with *have got to* for these situations.

a *You've got to fasten your seat belt now.*

3 Translation

Write these sentences in your own language.

a We haven't got to change offices.

b Have you got to wait for her?

c When have they got to be in Madrid?

d I've got to pay the bill.

Reference

We use **have got to** to express obligation. It means that something is necessary.

EXAMPLES: ***I've got to*** *go to the dentist.*
(I've got an appointment.)

I haven't got to *go now.*
(My appointment is later.)

Positive statements

I/You/We/They	have	
She/He/It	has	got to go.

Negative statements

I/You/We/They	haven't have not	
She/He/It	hasn't has not	got to go.

Questions

Have I/you/we/they	
Has he/she/it	got to go?

Have to means the same as **have got to** in British English, when we are speaking. **Have to** is more common in written English. The negative form **don't have to** is also common in spoken English.

EXAMPLES: *We **have to** make arrangements now.*
*You **don't have to** start today.*
***Does** she **have to** write a report?*

60

Present continuous for the future

Practice

1 Make sentences about future plans. Use present continuous verb forms.

a I leave / this job / on Friday.
I'm leaving this job on Friday.

b the trip / finish tomorrow.

c the receptionist / start on Monday.

d they / have a meeting at the beginning of next week.

e the director / open the new building this afternoon.

f you / come this evening?

g he / work tonight?

h we / go to the party next weekend?

2 Answer these questions about yourself. Use the present continuous.

a What are you doing this evening?
I'm finishing my English homework, and then I'm going out with my friends.

b Where are you spending the weekend?

c Are you taking a holiday this year?

d Are you going to any parties in the next few weeks?

e When is your English course finishing?

f What are you doing at the end of the course?

3 Now write five more sentences about yourself. Use these time phrases.

a ... tomorrow.
I'm having a meeting with my boss tomorrow.

b ... in a week's time.

c ... soon.

d ... the week after next.

e ... this weekend.

4 Translation

Write these sentences in your own language.

a I'm talking to her tomorrow.

b I'm talking to her now.

c Is she having dinner with John on Saturday?

d Is she having dinner with John at the moment?

Reference

We often use the present continuous to refer to things happening now (*see Grammar backup 3*).

EXAMPLE: **I'm sending** a fax at the moment.

We also use the present continuous to talk about fixed plans for the future.

EXAMPLES: **I'm visiting** *my parents at the weekend.*
She's having *an interview tomorrow morning.*

Time phrases make this future reference clear.

EXAMPLES: *She's driving there* <u>next week</u>.
I'm seeing *her* <u>soon</u>.
I'm coming <u>tomorrow</u>.
It's starting <u>in two hours</u>.
They're closing <u>the day after tomorrow</u>.

The form of the present continuous to refer to the present and the future is exactly the same.

Publicity

8

- Find out about a publicity event
- Grammar:
    relative clauses with *who*
    and *which*

A publicity event

Discussion: a publicity event

1 **Look at the photograph on the right.**

a What can you see?

b Why do you think it is therè?

c How do you think people feel
   when they see something like
   this in the centre of town?

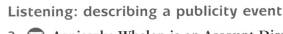

Listening: describing a publicity event

2 🔊 **Agnieszka Whelan is an Account Director with Burson-Marsteller
    in Warsaw. She is describing a publicity event for a company
    called FilmNet. Listen.**

a What is the name of the animal in the photograph above?

b Which building did they put it on?

c How long was it there?

d How big was it?

e What did people think about it?

f What happened on the evening of the last day?

Reading a newspaper article

3 **Read only the headline from the newspaper article on the next page.**

a *Ape* can be a noun (a kind of animal) or a verb (to act like another
   person or thing). Which is it here?

b Which phrase describes other international television companies?

c Which word means *goes*?

FILMNET APES THE BIG BOYS AS IT HEADS EAST

The official launch of FilmNet in Warsaw last week caught the imagination of the Polish capital by putting a 20-metre inflatable King Kong on top of the city's Palace of Culture.

5 Malgorzsta Potocki, who is one of Poland's leading independent television and film producers, shared the feelings of many Polish people: 'I don't believe it. It's absolutely perfect.' There was also a laser light show and a huge VIP party, which took place inside the palace.

10 'If you want to do business in a new market, you have to let people know that you exist,' a spokesperson said. 'When you do something like this, everybody notices.'

FilmNet is applying for a cable licence. It hopes that its publicity will persuade politicians and attract the 15 Polish television audience. The satellite channel, which has its head office in Stockholm, began a 12-hour programme of films and top Italian and English football on November 1st.

There are 1.5 million homes with satellite television 20 in Poland. FilmNet has about 700,000 customers at the moment in Scandinavia, Belgium, Luxembourg and the Netherlands. The service in Poland will cost about $12 a month and will also be available in Hungary, the Czech Republic, Slovakia, Slovenia and Croatia.

4 Now read the article.

a What does FilmNet want to do in Poland?

b How do you think the event helped them?

5 Find these words or short forms in the text. What do you think they mean? Use a dictionary to check your answers.

launch (line 1) VIP (l. 9) market (l. 10)
spokesperson (l. 11) licence (l. 14) audience (l. 16)

Grammar: relative clauses with *who* and *which*

6 Look at these sentences and answer the questions.

A *FilmNet, who has customers in many countries, wants to sell its services in Poland.*

B *Danuta Janiurek, who lives in Warsaw, saw King Kong on her way to work.*

C *There was also a huge VIP party, which took place inside the palace.*

a If you take the underlined clause away, is each sentence complete?

b We can combine two simple sentences by using a relative clause with *who* or *which*. Make two sentences from each of the sentences A – C.

c When does a relative clause begin with *which*? When does it begin with *who*?

d How are relative clauses separated from the rest of the sentence?

7 Complete the relative clauses with *who* or *which*.

a He's visiting his sister, ... lives near Warsaw.

b The company, ... is Swedish, wants to do business in Poland.

c The office is near the station, ... is next to the Palace of Culture.

d My boss, ... is Polish, speaks good English.

8 Write one sentence. Include information from the second sentence in a relative clause.

a The VIP party was very successful. It was inside the Palace of Culture.

 The VIP party, which was inside the Palace of Culture, was very successful.

b FilmNet wants to do business in Poland. Poland is a new market for the company.

c The service includes Italian and English football. It started on November 1st.

d The guests enjoyed the party very much. They saw a laser light show.

▶▶ p.68 **Grammar backup 8**

Speaking and Writing: a product launch

9 Discuss ideas for launching a new shampoo, cat food or pop music CD.

10 Write about your plans to launch the new product.

 EXAMPLE: *Our shampoo, which is called Hair First, is for young people. Young people watch a lot of television, so we want to...*

Action B Invitations

- Understand invitations
- Make a spoken invitation
- Write a business invitation
- Vocabulary:
  events

Reading invitations

1 Look at the three invitations below.

A

Mr Jósef Janowski, President of HCL representative office in Warsaw requests the pleasure of your company at a reception to celebrate the opening of the new HCL office in Poland.

The reception is on 12th January 1997 at 18.00 at the Central Hotel in Warsaw.

RSVP Helen Zak tel. (48 2) 619 99 00

B

TRAVIS ENGLISH BOOKSHOP

Travis English Bookshop would like to invite you to a lunch party to celebrate the publication of A DAY IN PARADISE, the new novel by ANDREW DITCH. Andrew will be available to sign copies.

Date: February 1st   Time: 12.00
Location: Hotel Iris, Brussels
Please reply to Ms K Verhaeven
on (2) 613 1187

C

COMPUTER ACE MAGAZINE welcomes you to its fifth annual International Computer Show.

Where? Cresta Exhibition
Centre, Glasgow.
When? Saturday and Sunday,
April 8th/9th
10.00 a.m. - 6.00 p.m.

Bring this ticket with you for FREE entry (value £20)

CAM Computer Ace Publishing

Which invitation:

a is from a new business?
b is from a company that has an event like this every year?
c suggests that there is a meal?
d is for an evening event?
e is for a weekend event?
f is for an event that is probably open to everyone?
g is written in very formal language?

Which invitations expect:

h an answer?
i you to buy something at the event?

2 **Complete this chart with words and phrases from the first sentence of each invitation.**

	the name of the person / company	the invitation	the reason for the event
A	Mr Jósef Janowski		
B		would like to invite you	
C			fifth annual International Computer Show

Vocabulary: events

3 Look at these different types of events.

a reception	a meeting	a party
a presentation	a talk	a demonstration
a seminar	a conference	an exhibition

Use a dictionary to help you. At which events is the main purpose to:

a sit down and discuss business?
b listen to someone giving information?
c meet people socially?
d see a lot of different products?

Listening and Speaking: making a spoken invitation

4 🔊 **A woman is inviting a colleague to dinner. Listen and read. How does:**

a Helena invite Paul and his wife?
b Paul say that they want to come very much?
c Helena suggest a day? (two expressions)
d Paul say that they can't come on Friday?

> *Helena:* Oh, Paul. Would you and Margaret like to come to dinner?
> *Paul:* Well, thanks. We'd love to. But when?
> *Helena:* How about Friday? John and I are free then.
> *Paul:* Hmm. Friday's difficult. I'm afraid we're busy.
> *Helena:* Oh, is Saturday possible?
> *Paul:* Yes, that's fine. Thanks very much.

5 Work in pairs. Use expressions from the Phrasebook.

A: Invite your partner to the events below. Continue the conversation until you agree a day and time.

B: Decide if you can go to the event. If you can, accept.

- a party
- lunch
- dinner
- an exhibition
- the theatre

Writing an invitation

6 Your boss asks you to write invitations for the following events. Use the invitations in Exercise 1 to help you.

a Your company: ABG Construction
Managing Director's name: Mr Sergio Ginetti
Event: party
Reason: to celebrate one year in Rome.
Invitation: formal (imagine a place, time and date)

b Your company: Delphi Books
Event: 'The National Book Exhibition' (an exhibition of books for a number of publishers)
Invitation: an invitation that is also a free ticket (imagine a place, time and date)

Talking point

PARTIES DON'T HELP THE BUSINESS. PEOPLE JUST COME FOR THE FREE FOOD AND DRINK.

What do *you* think?

Phrasebook

Spoken invitations

Would you like to come to dinner?
I'd/we'd love to.
I'd like to invite you to dinner.
Thank you very much.
How about Friday?
Friday's **difficult.**
I'm afraid we're busy on Friday.
Is Saturday **possible?**
That's fine.

Action C # Advertising campaigns

- Find out about an advertising campaign
- Vocabulary:
  advertising campaigns
- Grammar:
  possessive pronouns

Discussion: advertising campaigns

1 **How do advertisers persuade you to buy something? Look at the box below. Think of television and magazine advertisements that you know. Do you agree? Can you add anything to the list?**

> Advertisements are effective when:
> • you like the person in the advertisement.
> • you want to be like that person.
> • you agree with the argument in the advertisement.
> • you think the advertisement is funny.

2 **You want to advertise a credit card.**

a What features of a credit card do you want to tell people about?
b Most credit cards offer similar services. Can you present your credit card so that people prefer it to other cards?

Reading about an advertising campaign

3 **Read about Barclaycard's advertising campaign.**

a Why did Barclaycard launch a new advertising campaign in 1990?
b Which three features did this new card have?
c What kind of campaign did the advertising agency plan?

Barclaycard is a popular British credit card from Barclays Bank. Its main competitor is the Access card. Between 1979 and 1990, Access was more popular than Barclaycard, which lost money in 1990. That same year Barclaycard launched a card with new features with a very successful advertising campaign. By October 1991, theirs was the number one in Britain and Barclaycard were in profit again.

One of the features of the new card was free insurance. If you bought an item with a Barclaycard and something happened to it in the next hundred days, you got your money back.

Barclaycard asked an advertising agency, BMP DDB Needham, to design a new campaign. They wanted to show the public that Barclaycard: is accepted all over the world; offers free insurance; is replaced quickly if you lose it.

The agency made a number of television advertisements with amusing characters and story lines. They created Latham, an old-fashioned James Bond character who thinks he knows everything. They chose Rowan Atkinson, famous for his 'Mr Bean' character, to play this part. We always see Latham with his sensible assistant, Bough.

In one advertisement, Latham and Bough are in a market in North Africa. They go into a carpet shop. Latham buys a carpet with cash after arguing about the price. Bough buys a carpet too, but he pays for his with a Barclaycard. He tells Latham that it is insured. Latham laughs at him and says that very little can happen to a carpet. As he speaks, he rests one end of the carpet in a small fire by accident. 'Ah, smell those Tuareg camp fires – unmistakable,' says Latham, looking out across the desert.

4 Find these words in the text. What do you think they mean?

> popular   competitor   campaign   in profit
> the public   amusing   sensible

Use a dictionary to check your answers.

5 Say what you think.

a What features of the new Barclaycard does the advertisement try to show? Is it successful?

b Why do you think the advertising campaign was so successful? (Look at your list from Exercise 1.)

Grammar: possessive pronouns

6 Look at the two sentences from the text. Answer the questions below.

A *By October 1991, <u>theirs</u> was the number one card in Britain and Barclaycard were in profit again.*

B *Bough buys a carpet too, but he pays for <u>his</u> with a Barclaycard.*

a In A, what does *theirs* refer to?

b In B, what does *his* refer to?

c Are the underlined words followed by nouns?

7 Complete the chart with possessive adjectives and possessive pronouns.

possessive adjectives (followed by a noun)		possessive pronouns (in place of a noun)
It's **my** car.	➝	It's **mine.**
It's ..... car.	➝	It's **yours.**
It's **his** car.	➝	It's ..... .
It's ..... car.	➝	It's **hers.**
It's ..... car.	➝	It's **ours.**
It's **their** car.	➝	It's ..... .

8 Read this conversation. Then complete it with possessive adjectives and possessive pronouns.

> A: Whose car is that outside?
> B: Which car? The green one?
> A: Yes.
> B: It's (a) ..... .
> A: (b) ..... ? Are you sure? I thought (c) ..... car was red.
> B: No. I sold that. Let me have a look. Oh, no. That's not (d) ..... car.
> A: Whose is it then?
> B: Perhaps it's Sandra's.
> A: No, (e) ..... is blue.
> B: What about those two men in the meeting? Maybe it's (f) ..... .

▶▶ p.69   **Grammar backup 8**

Speaking about advertisements

9 Think of a popular advertisement. Describe it but don't give the name of the product. Ask other people to guess the name.

Word file   Unit 8

EVENTS
conference
demonstration
exhibition
launch
party
presentation
reception
seminar
talk

INVITATIONS
celebrate
invitation
invite

pleasure
request
RSVP

PEOPLE
audience
public
spokesperson
VIP

OTHER
amusing
ape
cable
campaign

competitor
feature
insurance
novel
popular
profit
publicity
satellite
sensible

Relative clauses with *who* and *which*

Practice

1 Complete these sentences with *who* or *which*.

a Jane, *who* is our marketing manager, speaks French well.

b The train, ... leaves from Central Station, goes all the way to Amsterdam.

c FilmNet, ... has a lot of customers in northern Europe, wants to attract Polish customers.

d Big parties, ... cost a lot of money, are not always the best launch events.

e My husband, ... works in marketing, promotes new products on the Internet.

2 Write one sentence. Use a relative clause to include information from the second sentence.

a This is John. He is starting his new job tomorrow.
   This is John, who is starting his new job tomorrow.

b I went to Tallinn. Tallinn is the capital of Estonia.

c My sister Elsa is coming with us. She's two years older than me.

d The manager of this department is only twenty-five. She's French.

e I complained about the food. It was terrible.

f The car park is full now. It was empty this morning.

3 Add a relative clause to these sentences.

a His new computer, *which is the latest model*, was very expensive.

b My brother, ..., works in a bank.

c Vienna, ..., is a good place for our new office.

d I like my colleagues, ...

4 Translation
   Write these sentences in your own language.

a I drive to my office, which is 10 kilometres from my house.

b Our products, which are all made in Europe, sell very well.

c We employ young people, who know more about computers than older people.

Reference

The relative clauses in this unit are called non-defining relative clauses. These clauses give extra information about people or things. They are separated from the rest of the sentence by commas. Non-defining relative clauses always start with a relative pronoun, like **who** or **which.**

We use **who** to add information about people.

EXAMPLE: *My friend, **who** is from Denmark, speaks four languages.*

We use **which** to add information about things.

EXAMPLE: *The company, **which** has its head office in Geneva, employs people from many countries.*

If we take a non-defining relative clause away from a sentence, the sentence is still complete. The most important information is still there.

EXAMPLE: *That man over there (, who I know very well,) works for the government.*

Non-defining relative clauses are common in formal writing. They are sometimes used in formal speech.

There is another type of relative clause – the defining relative clause. This is an important part of the sentence because it identifies people or things. It is not separated from the rest of the sentence by commas.

EXAMPLE: *I am writing to the woman who took my deposit.*

Possessive pronouns

Practice

1 Complete these sentences with possessive pronouns (*mine / hers*, etc.) or possessive adjectives (*my / her*, etc.)

a Whose office is this? Is it yours? (you)
b Is this ..... office? (you)
c This is not Kaz's coat. The brown one is ..... . (he)
d Excuse me. I think that is ..... seat. (I)
e We're having dinner at ..... hotel. (we)
f Where are they having .....? (they)
g That's not ..... ticket. (he) It's ..... . (she)
h There's someone in ..... (I) office, so can we use .....? (you)
i ..... name is Suzanna. (I) What's .....? (you)

2 Translation

Write these sentences in your own language.

a Hers is the house on the left.
b That's not his coat, it's mine.
c That's a Sony video camera – and that's one of theirs too.

Reference

We use possessive pronouns to answer the question **Whose ...?**

EXAMPLE: **Whose** desk is that?
It's **mine**.
It's **hers**.

possessive adjectives	possessive pronouns
my office ⟶	**mine**
your office ⟶	**yours**
his office ⟶	**his**
her office ⟶	**hers**
our office ⟶	**ours**
their office ⟶	**theirs**

Possessive pronouns are NOT used before nouns.

EXAMPLE: It's **mine** desk. ✗
It's **my** desk. ✓

We can also use **'s** after a noun or name to answer the question **Whose ...?**

EXAMPLES: It's Debbie**'s**.
It's my colleague**'s**.
(It's **hers**.)
It's John**'s**.
It's my friend**'s**.
(It's **his**.)

THAT'S OURS. AND THAT'S YOURS.

9

Action **A**

Olivetti

- ■ Read a company history
- ■ Understand bar charts
- ■ Vocabulary:
  stages in production
- ■ Grammar:
  comparative forms

Reading a company history

1 **What do you know about Olivetti? Can you answer these questions?**

a What does Olivetti do?
b Where is the head office?
c Who started the company?
d How is it different now from when it started?

2 **Read about Olivetti and check your answers to Exercise 1.**

A short history of Olivetti

The engineer Camillo Olivetti was 40 years old when he started the company in 1908. At his factory in Ivrea, he designed and produced the first Italian typewriter. Today the company headquarters are still in Ivrea, near Turin, but the company is much larger than it was in those days and there are offices all around the world.

The Olivetti M1 typewriter 1911

By 1930 there was a staff of 700 and the company produced 13,000 machines a year. Some went to customers in Italy, but Olivetti exported more typewriters to other countries.

Camillo's son, Adriano, started working for the company in 1924 and later he became the boss. He introduced a standard speed for the production line and he employed technology and design specialists. The company developed new and better typewriters and then calculators and accounting machines. In 1959 it produced the ELEA computer system. This was the first mainframe computer designed and manufactured in Italy.

The ELEA computer system 1959

After Adriano died in 1960, the company had a period of financial problems. Other manufacturers, especially the Japanese, made faster progress in electronic technology than the Italian company.

In 1978, Carlo de Benedetti became the new boss. Olivetti increased its distribution and service networks and made agreements with other companies to design and produce more sophisticated office equipment. Soon it became one of the world's leading companies in information technology and communications. There are now five independent companies in the Olivetti group – one for personal computers, one for other office equipment, one for systems and services, and two specialising in tele-communications.

Most of the Olivetti data in this book was gathered in 1994 and is for illustration only. It may not represent the reality of the group's activities today. The names and the photographs on page 72 are not of actual personnel.

3 **Look at the text again.**

a Find *in* (1908) and *by* (1930) in the text. What is the difference in meaning?

b Now find these words.

> when   later   then   after   soon

Which of the words above can you add to the first sentence below? Which words can you add to the second sentence?

- ..... he finished university, he joined his father's company.
- ..... he introduced new ideas to the company.

Vocabulary: stages in production

4 **Look at these verbs in the text.**

> design   produce   export   develop

a Which verb has a similar meaning to *manufacture*?

b Put the verbs in the same order as a factory process.

5 **Complete each sentence below with the correct form of one of these verbs.**

> introduce   employ   increase

a How many people do you .....?

b This year our sales are ..... .

c We want to ..... a new computer system.

Grammar: comparative forms

6 **Complete the chart with other comparative forms from the text.**

> EXAMPLE: ... *the company is much <u>larger</u> than it was* ...

		comparative forms
adjectives	large	larger
	fast	.....
	sophisticated	.....
	good	.....
quantities	few	fewer
	many / much	.....

7 **What do we add to short regular adjectives to make comparatives? What do we add to long adjectives?**

▶▶ p.76 **Grammar backup 9**

Reading: understanding bar charts

8 **Look at the bar chart and the article.**

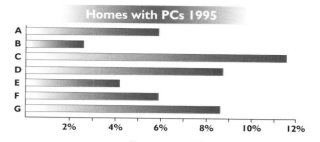

Homes with PCs 1995

PC World

11.5% of British households have a personal computer. This is a higher proportion than the rest of Europe. In Germany the figure is 8.7%, the Netherlands 8.6%, France 5.9%, Sweden 5.9%, Italy 4.2% and Spain 2.6%

a Match each bar A–G with a country.

b ▢ Listen and repeat these percentages.
- 2.6% (*two point six per cent*)
- 4.2% • 5.9% • 8.6% • 8.7% • 11.5%

9 **Complete the sentences about the chart with comparative forms of the words in brackets.**

a *More* British homes than Spanish homes had computers in 1995. (many)

b ..... Swedish homes than Dutch homes had computers. (few)

c Computers were ..... in French homes than in Italian homes at that time. (popular)

d There was a ..... percentage of home computers in Northern Europe than in Southern Europe. (high)

Writing: making comparisons

10 Look at this modern Olivetti computer. Write sentences comparing this computer with the typewriter on page 70.

Speaking: using computers

11 Ask other people in the class where, why and how often they use computers. Then discuss this information in pairs. Have you got similar information?

Action B

Company structure

Understand pie charts and graphs
■ **Vocabulary:**
  • **company departments**
  • **a factory process**
■ **Grammar:**
  question forms with and without *do / does / did*

Reading and Writing: understanding pie charts

1 Look at the two charts below.

a How many people work for Olivetti?
b What percentage of them work in Italy?
c What proportion of the staff:
  • work in factories?
  • design new products?
  • work with customers?
  • manage company business from offices?

Mr Molino
Purchasing

Mr Galiani
Mechanical Design

Mr Barbieri
Product Planning

Mr Foglietta
Financial Control

Mr Salvini
Quality Control

Mr Brunetti
Public Relations

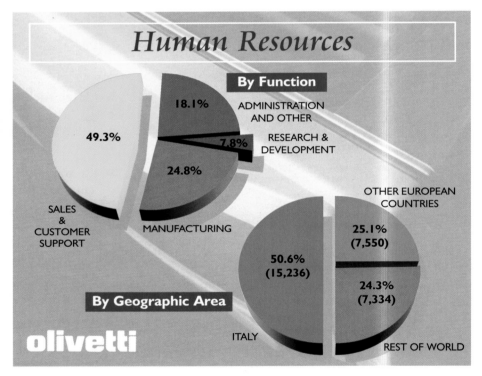

2 Compare the numbers of Olivetti staff in different jobs. Use *more* and *fewer*.

EXAMPLE: *More people work in Sales and Customer Support than in Research & Development.*
Fewer people work in R & D than in Manufacturing.

Vocabulary: company departments

3 Look at the pictures of some senior people in Olivetti, Italy. Use a dictionary to help you. Which department:

a advises all Olivetti's offices about commercial affairs? Financial Control
b explains to visitors what the company does?
c designs new parts for machines?
d tests new products?
e decides that a new product is necessary?
f buys parts for computers?

Grammar: questions with and without *do / does / did*

4 **Read these questions and answers.**

- Who welcomes visitors to Ivrea? Mr Brunetti.
- Who does he welcome? Visitors to Ivrea.
- What does Mr Brunetti talk about? The work of the company.
- What interests visitors? Olivetti's new products.

Complete the rules for question forms. Add *subject* or *object*.

In the question: *Who does he welcome?*
who is the ..... .
In the question: *Who welcomes visitors?*
who is the ..... .

5 📼 **Listen to a conversation about jobs in another company. Answer these questions.**

a Who does Mary work for?
b Who goes to a PLT party?
c Who sends routine invitations?
d Who do good food and drink attract?

6 **Look at the information about Olivetti staff in Exercise 3. Use the information to complete these questions.**

a Who ..... ? Mr Salvini.
  Who tests new products?
b What ..... ? He designs machine parts.
c Who ..... ? Staff at Olivetti's commercial offices.
d What ..... ? He buys parts for computers.

▶▶ p.77 **Grammar backup 9**

Vocabulary: a factory process

7 **Complete this chart. Which pair of words is different from the others?**

verb	noun
produce	product
design	....
control	.....
.....	test
.....	export

Reading: understanding graphs

8 **Look at the graph. Are the statements below true or false? Correct the false ones.**

a Olivetti earned more in 1995 than in 1994.
b 1992 was a better year than 1991.
c The company earned more than 9,000 billion lire in 1994.
d The earnings for 1991 were higher than for 1993.

9 **Complete these sentences with the correct year.**

a Olivetti's earnings fell by 6.8% in 1992.
b The company's earnings rose by 7.3% in ..... .
c The company's earnings rose to 9,076 billion lire in ..... .
d The company's earnings improved between ..... and 1995.

10 **Match each verb on the left with a definition on the right.**

a fall   • go down
b rise   • get better
c improve   • go up

Speaking and Writing: describing graphs

11 **Work in pairs. Discuss the graph below. What does it show?**

12 **Write five sentences about the company's sales in this period.**

Action **C** # New technology

- Read a project report
- Discuss new technology
- Vocabulary:
  security systems
- Grammar:
  superlative forms

Reading a project report

1 Read about one of Olivetti's projects and answer these questions.

a Where is the club?

b Which of the facilities on the right has the club got?

c What is an 'active badge'? How do you think it works?

The intelligent club:

357 SPA CLUB, Caracas

At the 357 Spa Club in the Venezuelan capital, members can play tennis and squash; they can swim in the pool and shoot in the shooting gallery; they can use the sauna and gymnasium; they can eat, drink and shop.

Olivetti has designed systems for the club with all the software applications in one control room. From the control room staff can find other members of staff, watch club rooms on video monitors and check other systems. These include the control of light, heat, air conditioning and security. People without special 'active badges' cannot enter the building.

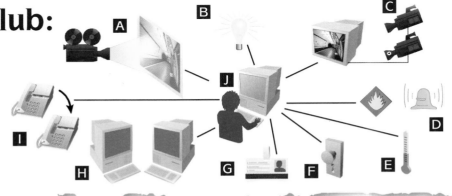

2 Match the pictures in the diagram with these labels. Use a dictionary to help you.

a temperature control
b telephone re-routing
c video surveillance
d lighting economy
e video entertainment

f doors access
g fire detection and alarm
h active badge
i system workstations and equipment
j control centre

Which parts of the system make the club safer for members?

Grammar: superlative forms

3 Read the comments about the club. Complete the table with superlative forms.

IT'S THE MOST IMPRESSIVE USE OF TECHNOLOGY I KNOW.

I THINK IT'S THE BEST CLUB IN TOWN BECAUSE IT'S THE SAFEST.

I USE THE CLUB BECAUSE IT HAS THE MOST FACILITIES. IT CERTAINLY ISN'T THE CHEAPEST.

		superlative forms
adjectives	safe	the safest
	cheap	.....
	impressive	.....
	good	.....
quantities	few	the fewest
	many / much	.....

 p.76 Grammar backup 9

Writing: comparing security systems

4 **Look at the security systems below. What kind of building are they best for? Write five sentences.**

- video surveillance • unarmed guards
- guard dogs • high fences • armed guards
- an alarm system

EXAMPLE: *Video surveillance is the most useful security system for a school, but it is also the most expensive.*

Discussion: technology

5 **Look at the photographs from Thailand and Kenya.**

B

A

a Describe what you see in each picture.

b Do these situations surprise you? Why / why not?

c What modern technology do you use at home and for your work or studies? What technology would you like to use?

d Do you think modern technological progress makes people more or less equal?

Use expressions from the Phrasebook to give opinions.

Phrasebook

Giving opinions

I think you can have too much information.
In my opinion, modern technology is too expensive for most people.
In my experience, television is still the best way to get information.
For me, the Internet is very exciting.

Word file Unit 9

DEPARTMENTS	produce	TIME
administration	product	after
design	test	by (1930)
development		in (1908)
financial control	**SALES**	later
head office	fall	soon
headquarters	improve	then
planning	increase	when
production	rise	
purchasing		**OTHER**
quality control	**SECURITY**	bar chart
research	access	graph
sales	alarm system	impressive
services	(un)armed guard	pie chart
	control centre	safe
PRODUCTION	fire detection	
design	security system	
develop	video surveillance	
export	workstation	

Comparative and superlative forms

Practice

1   Write the sentences in the correct order.

a   faster / e-mail / letters / is / than

b   than / planes / are / slower / trains

c   expensive / typewriters / than / are / computers / more

d   economical / a / car / less / is / small / car / big / a / than

e   secretaries / more / earn / managers / than / money / usually

2   Choose two cities and write about them. Use comparative forms of the <u>underlined</u> words.

a   <u>large</u>
    London is larger than Vienna.

b   <u>attractive</u>

c   <u>good</u> transport system

d   <u>warm</u> weather

e   <u>friendly</u> people

3   Write questions for these answers. Use superlative adjectives. Use the words in brackets to help you.

a   China. A quarter of all the people in the world lives there. (big / population)
    Which country has got the biggest population in the world?

b   Antarctica. The temperature is often about –57°C. (low / temperature)

c   The cheetah, a member of the cat family. It can run at 100km an hour. (fast / animal)

d   An American taxi-driver called Jon Minnoch (1941–83). He weighed 442kg. (heavy / man)

e   Zhang. There are about 113 million people with this surname in China. (common / surname)

4   Translation
    Write these sentences in your own language.

a   London is bigger than many European capitals.

b   It is one of the most expensive cities in Europe.

c   She earns less money than me and she does more work.

d   This is the worst job of them all.

Reference

We use comparative adjectives when we compare two things. We use superlative adjectives when we compare three or more things.

Short adjectives

adjective	comparative	superlative
high	high**er**	the high**est**
low	low**er**	the low**est**
big	big**ger**	the big**gest**
large	larg**er**	the larg**est**
dry	dri**er**	the dri**est**
happy	happ**ier**	the happ**iest**
good	**better**	the **best**
bad	**worse**	the **worst**
little	**less**	the **least**

EXAMPLES: *His salary is **higher** (**than** mine).*
          *Our sales figures are **the highest** (**of** all the sales figures).*

Long adjectives

adjective	comparative	superlative
careful	more/less careful	the most/ least careful
interesting	more/less interesting	the most/ least interesting

EXAMPLES: *My job is **more interesting than** yours.*
          *She is **the most careful** driver in the company.*

Note that some two-syllable adjectives (e.g. adjectives ending in -**y**) form comparatives with -**er** and superlatives with -**est**. Most other two-syllable adjectives add **more** and **most**, but some can have either form.

Quantities

We use these words with countable nouns.

| many | **more** | (the) **most** |
| few | few**er** | (the) few**est** |

EXAMPLE: *I'd like **more / fewer** responsibilities.*

We use these words with uncountable nouns.

| much | **more** | (the) **most** |
| little | **less** | (the) **least** |

EXAMPLE: *He does the **most / least** work.*

Questions with and without *do / does / did*

Practice

1 Look at each picture. Complete the questions with the correct past tense verb form.

a Who / Rolf? (love)
Penny.
Who did Rolf love?

b Who / James? (tell)
Sue.

c Who / Penny? (kill)
James.

d Who / Sue? (kiss)
James.

e Who / James? (arrest)
A police officer.

2 Answer these questions about yourself. Write complete sentences.

a Where do you live?
b Who lives with you?
c Which room do you study in?
d What helps you study?
e Who cooks in your house?
f What do you cook?

3 Write questions. Use these words to help you.

a What / do?
What do you do?
b Who / work / in the same office?
c Which jobs / like?
d Who / answer / the telephone?
e Which department / pay / you?

Reference

(subject)   (object)
↓   ↓
Pete wants more money.

Question words as subject

EXAMPLES: **Who** works here?
       Sue does. (Who / Sue = subject)

       Which department controls finance?
       Financial Control does. (Which department / Financial Control = subject)

Question words as object

EXAMPLES: **Who** did you see?
       I saw **John**. (Who / John = object)

       What do you do?

       Which cakes does she like?

4 Translation
Write these sentences in your own language.

a Who does John like?
b Who likes John?
c Which machine do you use?
d Which machine uses more electricity?

'WHAT COOKED YOU?'

Action **A**

Assembly lines

- Find out about a production process
- Describe a process
- Describe a sequence of events
- Vocabulary:
  - machine parts
  - sequence words
- Grammar:
  present simple passive

Reading and Listening: a production process

1 Look at the picture of a computer assembly line in an Olivetti factory.

a What factories are there in your area?

b What jobs do people do there?

2 Olivetti and Canon work together to produce photocopiers at a factory near Ivrea. Use these words to label the parts of a copier and the packaging. Use a dictionary to help you.

main body	internal components	outside panel	glass
plastic sheet	paper tray	manual	polystyrene	lid

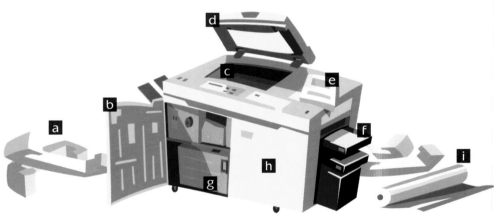

3 📠 **Listen and read. This is a description of part of the production process. Are these sentences true or false?**

a They make the components in this factory.

b Machines put the components into the main body.

c A computer checks each copier.

d They add the panels and glass when the machine is working well.

> The main body of the machine and the components are brought in from other factories. Some of the components are imported – from Japan, for example. In the factory here, the components are put in the machine by hand, and then all the functions of the photocopier are checked by computer. If there's a problem, the machines are repaired immediately. After that, the outside panels are added, and the glass for the top of the machine is put in place. Then the copiers are packed into boxes.

Grammar: present simple passive

4 **Look again at the interview extract in Exercise 3.**

a Find present passive verb forms (*be* + past participle).

EXAMPLE: *The copiers are packed into boxes.*

b What are the past participles of these verbs?

> **Regular:** import   check   repair   add
> **Irregular:**   bring   put

c Does the text tell us who or what:
  • makes the components?
  • checks the copiers?
  • puts the components in?
  • adds the panels and glass?
  Why / why not?

d Write one word to complete each sentence:
  • Copiers are ..... by Olivetti.
  • Each copier ..... checked in the factory.
  • Some components are produced ..... the Japanese.

5 **Look at the diagram on the right.**

a What is the past participle of each verb? Use the verbs to write a description of the stages in the process.

EXAMPLE: *The copier is wrapped in plastic.*

b Listen to a description of the same process and compare it with your description.

▶▶ p.84 **Grammar backup 10**

Writing and Speaking: describing a process

6 **Look at these words and expressions.**

> after that   and then   then   after   before

Complete each sentence with a word or expression to show the time sequence.

a Each copier is packed in polystyrene ..... it is put in a box.

b ..... the manual is added, the box is closed.

c The copiers are loaded onto a truck. ..... they are transported to distributors.

7 **Think of a process that you know about (e.g. how letters are delivered). Then work in pairs. Ask your partner about stages in his / her process. Use expressions from the Phrasebook.**

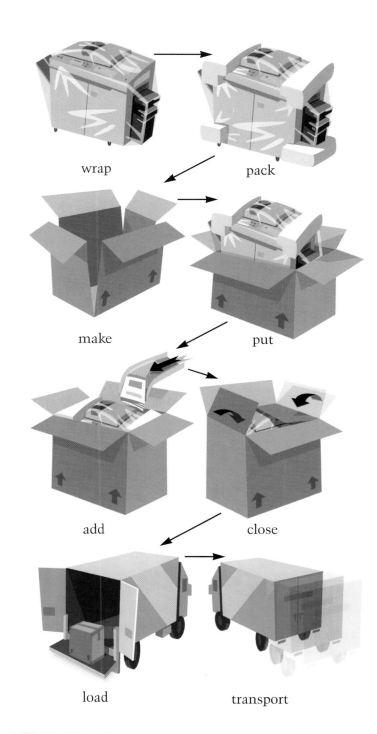

wrap   pack

make   put

add   close

load   transport

Phrasebook

Asking about processes

What's the first stage?
What happens next?
And then?
And after that?
At what stage is the manual added?

Action **B** # Making it clear

- Read about creating a new product
- Vocabulary:
  - general and specific descriptions
  - expressions with *do* or *make*
  - verbs of movement

Vocabulary: general and specific descriptions

1 **Look at the three pairs of pictures.**

a In each pair, which person is more helpful? Why?

b Can you think of a situation when it is useful to use the general words?

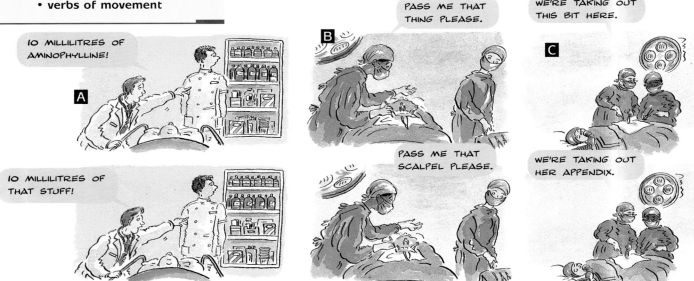

2 **Match these general words with the definitions below.**

stuff   thing   bit

- an object
- a part of an object
- an uncountable substance or a number of objects

3 **These words are a little less general than the words above.**

component   liquid   gas   tool   machine

a Look in your dictionary and check their meanings.

b Use the words to ask and answer about the pictures below. Use expressions from the Phrasebook.

EXAMPLE: *What do you call this machine?*
It's a printer.

Phrasebook

Asking for the right word

What do you call this thing / machine?
What's this stuff / liquid **called?**
What's the name for this bit / component?

printer

screwdriver

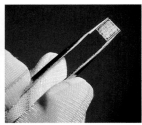
carbon monoxide

microchip

oil

Reading: creating a new product

4 Read about the creation of a new Olivetti product. Complete the chart below with past participles from the text.

When a request for a new product (for example, a smaller notebook) is received from the market, the concept is discussed first of all with the marketing department. A general idea is given to the design consultant, who does the drawings. Then the practical side is considered by the design department and the final idea is taken to the top managers. If they agree, a model is made. A prototype is created and tested, and then limited production is started.

infinitive	past participle
receive	received
discuss	.....
consider	.....
create	.....
test	.....
start	.....
give	.....
take	.....
make	.....

5 Look at these expressions with *do* and *make*.

do drawings   make a model
do market research   make a prototype

a How do you translate them into your language? Are there different verbs for *do* and *make*?
b Which verb do you think we use with these phrases?

a cup of tea   some repairs   your homework
computers

6 Complete these sentences with the correct form of *do* or *make*. Use a dictionary to help you.
a Sorry – I ..... a mistake!
b Can I ..... an appointment please?
c We like ..... business with you.
d She's ..... a phone call.
e When can we ..... some exercise?

Vocabulary: verbs of movement

7 Look at the diagram. Are the movements in the sentences below *towards* or *away from* the factory?

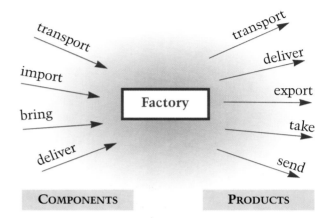

COMPONENTS   PRODUCTS

a We import components.
b Lorries bring the components here.
c Our lorries deliver computers to local agents.
d Olivetti exports many of its products.
e We send invoices to our customers.

Which actions can you also do on foot, with a parcel in your hand?

8 Complete these sentences with the correct form of one of the verbs above. More than one verb is possible.
a We ..... games from Korea.
b Can you ..... me last year's report please?
c Please ..... this letter to the post office.
d They ..... coffee to Europe.
e The lorries are ..... these goods to shops tomorrow.

Writing and Speaking: creating a new product

9 Look at these stages in the creation of a new product.

- advertise the new product
- order components
- decide the price
- name the product
- design the assembly line
- do market research
- start production
- design the product
- make a prototype

Write sentences about the order of the different stages. Use the present simple passive and *before / after*.

EXAMPLE: *The market research is done after the model is made.*

10 Which stage in the creation of a new product interests you most? Explain why.

Action **C**

- Read and write a company profile
- Grammar:
    past simple passive

Company profiles

Reading: Cadbury Schweppes

1 Can you name any of Cadbury Schweppes' products? Do you buy any of them?

2 Look at this article about Cadbury Schweppes. Why are these dates important in the history of the company?
  - the 1790s • 1799 • the 1830s • 1905 • 1969

Cadbury Schweppes plc

Cadbury Schweppes plc is one of the oldest and largest family businesses in the world today. Cadbury Limited merged with the drinks company Schweppes Limited in 1969, but the new company is still run by a member of the Cadbury family. It is a leading producer of chocolate and soft drinks. 5

The business was started by John Cadbury, who began making chocolate in the 1830s. He was joined in 1847 by his brother, Benjamin, and then John's sons continued the business. A new factory was opened in 1879 and two years later the company began to export its products. Cadbury's Dairy Milk, a milk chocolate bar, 10 was introduced in 1905 and remains popular now. In 1922 the Cadbury Brothers started to manufacture products overseas and after the Second World War the company was still the most successful chocolate manufacturer in Britain. The company was also known for its advanced working conditions and for the comfortable 15 houses that were built around its factory outside Birmingham for people of all classes.

Schweppes Limited was named after Jacob Schweppe, who was born in Germany but later moved to Britain. He started producing mineral water in the 1790s. The 20 company was sold in 1799 but the name was kept by the new owners. New products were introduced – other soft drinks such as tonic water and lemonade, and later jams and tea.

After the merger of the two companies, Cadbury 25 Schweppes bought a number of foreign companies and in 1995 became the third-largest soft drink company in the United States. Soft drinks and confectionery have been at the centre of its business activities since the eighties and it is now a major global company selling its products in over 190 countries around the world. 30

3 Find these words and expressions in the article. What do you think they mean? Use a dictionary to check your answers.
family businesses (lines 1 – 2)   merged (l. 2)   run (l. 4)
soft drinks (l. 5)   chocolate bar (l. 10)   owners (l. 22)
merger (l. 25)   confectionery (l. 28)   global company (l. 29 – 30)

Grammar: past simple passive

4 **Look at the article again.**

a Paragraph 1. Find:
  • a present tense verb.
  • a present passive verb.
  • a past tense verb.

b Paragraph 2. Look at part of this sentence:
  The business was started by John Cadbury ...
  • Who started the company?
  • How do we form the past simple passive?

  Find five past passive verbs in this paragraph.

c Paragraph 3. Who do you think:
  • named the company?
  • sold the company?
  • introduced new products?

  Why does the article not give us this information?

 p.85 **Grammar backup 10**

Writing: a company profile

5 **Look at the notes on the right about another successful company. Discuss possible verb forms to express each piece of information. Is it:**

a present or past?
b active or passive?

6 **Write about the Coca-Cola Company. Show your article to another person and ask for comments. Make changes to your article if you can improve it.**

Talking point

What do *you* think?

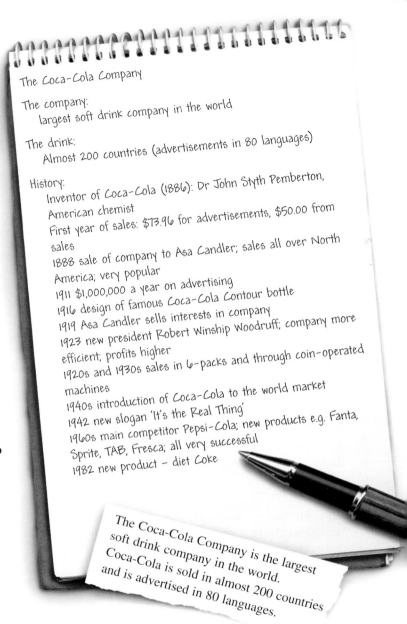

The Coca-Cola Company

The company:
  largest soft drink company in the world

The drink:
  Almost 200 countries (advertisements in 80 languages)

History:
  Inventor of Coca-Cola (1886): Dr John Styth Pemberton, American chemist
  First year of sales: $73.96 for advertisements, $50.00 from sales
  1888 sale of company to Asa Candler; sales all over North America; very popular
  1911 $1,000,000 a year on advertising
  1916 design of famous Coca-Cola Contour bottle
  1919 Asa Candler sells interests in company
  1923 new president Robert Winship Woodruff; company more efficient; profits higher
  1920s and 1930s sales in 6-packs and through coin-operated machines
  1940s introduction of Coca-Cola to the world market
  1942 new slogan 'It's the Real Thing'
  1960s main competitor Pepsi-Cola; new products e.g. Fanta, Sprite, TAB, Fresca; all very successful
  1982 new product – diet Coke

The Coca-Cola Company is the largest soft drink company in the world. Coca-Cola is sold in almost 200 countries and is advertised in 80 languages.

Word file Unit 10

GENERAL WORDS	PRODUCTION	OTHER
bit	add	advertise
component	assembly line	family business
gas	deliver	global company
liquid	import	manual
machine	load	market research
stuff	pack	merge
thing	transport	merger
tool	wrap	model
		owner
MACHINE PARTS	**PEOPLE**	polystyrene
body	consultant	prototype
panel	distributor	slogan
tray	inventor	truck
	manufacturer	

Grammar *backup 10*

Present simple passive

Practice

1 Write the past participles of these verbs.

a sell *sold*   b arrive   c deliver
d export   e repair   f do

2 Write answers to the questions using a passive form of the verb. Add any other words that you think are necessary.

a Why does Olivetti make typewriters in Brazil?
typewriters / sell / there
Because a lot of typewriters are sold there.

b How do foreign musical instruments arrive in Britain?
they / transport / air or sea

c How does new equipment arrive at the factory?
it / deliver / truck

d Do you sell all your products in this country?
a lot / export

e What happens if this machine breaks?
it / repair / a service company

f Do you do repairs in people's homes?
repairs / do / our workshop

3 Rewrite these sentences. Put the <u>underlined</u> words at the beginning and use the present simple passive.

a About half a million people read <u>the International Herald Tribune</u>.
The International Herald Tribune is read by about half a million people.

b They print <u>the newspaper</u> in eleven different cities.

c They sell <u>it</u> all over the world.

d They do not allow <u>children</u> into bars in Britain.

e Japan manufactures <u>a lot of electronic components</u>.

f Britain imports <u>huge amounts of electronic equipment</u> from Japan.

g People drink <u>millions of bottles of Coca-Cola</u> every day.

h The company advertises <u>the drink</u> on television and in cinemas.

4 Translation

Write these sentences in your own language.

a Drawings are done by a design consultant.

b Where is paper produced?

c The products are loaded into trucks and delivered immediately.

Reference

In an active sentence, the subject performs the action.

EXAMPLE: **We make** cars.

We use passive forms when:
• the action is more important than the person who does it.
• we do not know who does the action.

EXAMPLE: Cars **are made** here.

We use **by** if we want to include the person who does the action.

EXAMPLE: Some components are made **by** other companies.

The present simple passive

am / is / are + past participle

EXAMPLES: **is (not) advertised**
          are (not) taken

Past participles

Regular verbs: we form the past participle of regular verbs by adding **(e)d**.

EXAMPLES: transport**ed**
          receive**d**

Irregular verbs: *(see verb table, page 119)*

Past simple passive

Practice

1 Look at this newspaper report. Use the reporter's notes below to continue it.

The terrible storm that hit the south coast last night caused destruction and chaos to the small town of Tenby. One person ...

- storm last night
- one person killed
- thirty people injured
- hundreds of buildings damaged
- trees and telephone lines blown down
- four beach shops completely destroyed

2 Write questions using the past simple passive.

a When / package / deliver?
When was the package delivered?
b How many / computers / export / last year?
c Why / the company / sell?
d How much / the managing director / pay / last year?
e When / the room / clean?
f When / this report / write?
g Who / this report / write by?
h Where / those products / manufacture?

3 Translation

Write these sentences in your own language.

a I was born in Spain.
b Was she told about the new job?
c How were they sent? By road?
d Wasn't she introduced to the new boss?
e The components were manufactured in Japan but the machines weren't built there.

Reference

The past simple passive is often found in official reports and in newspaper reports.

We use it when:
- the action is more important than the person who did it.
- we do not know who did the action.

EXAMPLES: *Twenty people* **were injured** *last night.*
The company **was sold** *in 1995.*

The past simple passive

was / were + past participle

EXAMPLES: **was (not) killed**
were (not) taken

WHERE WERE YOU BORN?

11

- Use formal and informal language in telephone calls, memos and messages
- Grammar:
  will

The personal touch

Speaking: formal or informal?

1 Which of these phrases do we usually use with business contacts:

a that we know well?
b that we don't know well?
c in speech?
d in writing?

- Hi!
- Good morning.
- How are things?
- How's the family?
- Thank you for your order.
- Thank you for your letter of July 16th.
- Goodbye.
- Bye for now.
- I look forward to hearing from you.
- Please let me know as soon as you can.
- I would be grateful for a reply as soon as possible.
- Speak to you soon!
- Yours faithfully
- Best wishes
- Regards

Listening and Speaking: telephone talk

2 🔊 **Listen to two people talking about their telephone conversations with business contacts and answer the questions.**

Véronique Feldmann

a When she calls someone, what does she talk about first?
b Why does she do this?

Yveline Cochennec

c What does she talk about first?
d What language does she use for this?
e Why does she change languages in the middle of a conversation?

3 Work in pairs. Match each question with a possible response.

a Hi, Paul. How are things?
b How's the family?
c Did you have a good weekend?
d What did you do?
e When are you next coming to Paris?

- Yes, thanks. It was great.
- Fine, thanks. How are you?
- In about a month, I think.
- They're all well, thanks. How's Jean-Claude?
- Oh, we went skiing.

4 Imagine that you and your partner do business with each other. Decide:

a what your area of business is.

b why you often speak to each other on the telephone.

c what you know about each other's personal lives.

Have a telephone conversation. Start with friendly personal chat and then talk about business.

Reading memos

5 Look at the top part of each of these notes.

MEMORANDUM

To: Penny Klapp   Date: 1st May
        Tim Hodges
cc: Lara Thatcher

From: Howard Colley

Re: Planning Meeting

There will be a meeting in my office at 9.00 a.m. tomorrow.
We will probably have time to discuss next year's diary too.

MEMO

To: All staff
From: James Wilton
Subject: Staff Meeting

I hope you're all feeling relaxed after your holiday! We'll
have a meeting tomorrow at 2 p.m. to talk about new
projects. I'm afraid it probably won't end until about 6 p.m.
so will you try not to be late?!

a What is the short form of *memorandum*?

b Is Lara invited to the planning meeting? What does *cc* mean?

c Which two words introduce the reasons for the notes?

6 Look at the messages in each note.

a Which message is friendlier and less formal? How do you know?

b Are the notes about past or future meetings? Which words and phrases tell us this?

Grammar: *will*

7 Look again at the memos in Exercise 5.

a Which of these can follow *will* in a sentence?
   • to be   • being   • be

b What is the short form of *will not*?

c Look at the position of *probably* in these phrases:
   • will probably be   • will be probably
   • probably will be
   Which is the best position?

d Now look at these negative phrases. Which is the best position for *probably*?
   • won't probably be   • won't be probably
   • probably won't be

8 Look at the pictures of James Wilton's staff now. Which people will be at the meeting tomorrow, do you think? Where will the others be? Use *probably*, *certainly* and *definitely*.

Frank

Sally and Mike

Madge

Pat

Lara

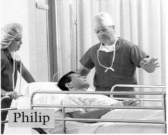
Philip

 p.92   Grammar backup 11

Writing a note

9 You are Madge. You have a doctor's appointment tomorrow. Write an informal note to James Wilton about the meeting. Explain why you won't be there.

Action **B**

It's not all business

- Respond to a telephone caller
- Apologise, ask for information and make suggestions on the telephone
- Vocabulary:
  - telephone expressions
  - personal qualities

Speaking and Listening: telephone manners

1 Work in pairs. Look at the pictures and questions a – d. What do you think the answers to the questions are?

A

YES, IT IS. I'M HER NEW ASSISTANT, TOM DRYSDALE. HER LAST ASSISTANT LEFT TO HAVE A BABY ...

TOMORROW. LET'S SEE. WHAT'S THE DATE TOMORROW? OH, YES, HERE WE ARE. MRS FOYLE. ACTUALLY, MRS PANE WILL BE PLEASED ABOUT THAT BECAUSE SHE WANTS TO GO TO THE HAIRDRESSER'S, AND ...

GOODBYE.

B

THAT'S RIGHT.

HE'S NOT HERE.

AT ABOUT FIVE O'CLOCK.

C

CERTAINLY. COULD YOU GIVE ME YOUR NAME, PLEASE?

RIGHT, MR BUSH. WOULD NEXT TUESDAY BE CONVENIENT? AT ELEVEN O'CLOCK?

THANK YOU, MR BUSH. GOODBYE.

a Why is each caller phoning?
b How does each caller feel about the conversation?
c What is each caller saying? Recreate the conversations.
d 🔊 Listen to the conversations. Compare them with yours.

Vocabulary: personal qualities

2 The telephone calls in Exercise 1 are short business calls with strangers.

a Which assistant from Exercise 1 would you like to speak to?
b What impression did the assistants give to the callers? Use these adjectives to describe the assistants. Use a dictionary to help you.

warm cold confident nervous (un)friendly (un)cooperative (un)professional (un)helpful (in)discreet (in)efficient calm hostile clear confused

3 Work in pairs. Practise the three conversations again, but change them so that the assistant sounds friendly, confident and efficient, and the caller is happy.

Speaking: making telephone calls

4 Match each heading (a – f) on the left with three phrases on the right.

a Answering the telephone

b Asking someone to wait

c Ending the conversation

d Apologising

e Asking for the caller's name

f Making a suggestion

- Just a moment. **b**
- Bye then.
- I'm afraid (she's in a meeting).
- Could you hold on a moment, please?
- Hang on ...
- Who's that?
- Would you like to call later?
- Hi. Sandy speaking ...
- Shall I get him / her to give you a ring?
- I'm terribly sorry.
- Hello. Clearview Ltd.
- Good morning. How can I help you?
- Goodbye. Thank you for calling.
- Oh dear ... sorry!
- Could you tell me your name, please?
- You can try again this afternoon.
- Goodbye.
- And your name is ...?

Talking point

BUILDING PERSONAL RELATIONSHIPS IS A WASTE OF COMPANY TIME AND MONEY.

What do *you* think?

5 Look at the three phrases you have for each heading. Decide which phrase is:

a very formal and polite, for people you do not know.

b less formal and more neutral, for people you do not know very well.

c informal and friendly, for people you know.

6 Work in pairs. Use some of the expressions in Exercise 4 to have telephone conversations. Look at the situations below, or imagine a different situation.

Situation 1

A: You are the caller. You want to speak to the Sales Manager. It is the first time you have called this company.

B: You are the Personal Assistant to the Sales Manager. You answer the telephone. Be very formal and polite and explain that the Sales Manager is in a meeting. Ask if the caller wants to leave a message.

Situation 2

A: You are Jennifer Prentice's Personal Assistant. Jennifer is in her office but she does not want any calls at all! You know the caller very well but you must not tell him / her that Jennifer is in her office. Make an excuse and ask if you can help or take a message.

B: You telephone Jennifer Prentice, the Marketing Manager. You know her assistant well.

Action **C**

Putting things right

- Read and write faxes
- Apologise, explain and suggest solutions in correspondence
- Grammar:
  articles

Reading faxes

1 Read the two faxes below and answer these questions.

a What is the problem? What is the suggested solution?

b Which company is supplying the parts? Which company wants the parts?

c How many people will receive copies of fax A?

d Look at the reference after *Interspeed UK* in fax A. Next time Interspeed faxes JAC the reference will be different. What will it be? Why?

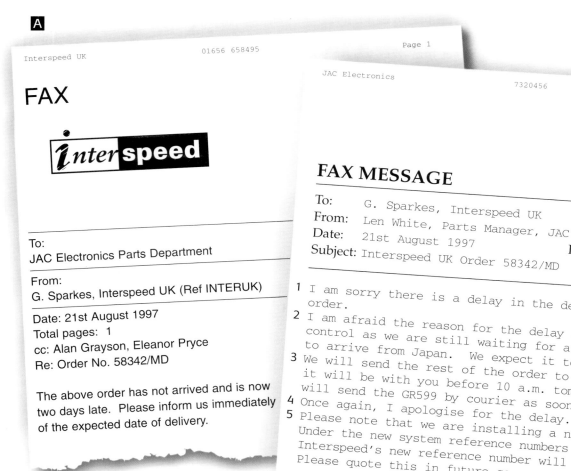

A

Interspeed UK   01656 658495

FAX

To:
JAC Electronics Parts Department

From:
G. Sparkes, Interspeed UK (Ref INTERUK)

Date: 21st August 1997
Total pages: 1
cc: Alan Grayson, Eleanor Pryce
Re: Order No. 58342/MD

The above order has not arrived and is now two days late. Please inform us immediately of the expected date of delivery.

B

Page 1

JAC Electronics

7320456

Page 1

FAX MESSAGE

JAC ELECTRONICS

To: G. Sparkes, Interspeed UK
From: Len White, Parts Manager, JAC Electronics
Date: 21st August 1997
Subject: Interspeed UK Order 58342/MD   Pages: 1

1 I am sorry there is a delay in the delivery of the above order.

2 I am afraid the reason for the delay is beyond our control as we are still waiting for a component (GR599) to arrive from Japan. We expect it to be here tomorrow.

3 We will send the rest of the order to you immediately and it will be with you before 10 a.m. tomorrow morning. We will send the GR599 by courier as soon as it reaches us.

4 Once again, I apologise for the delay.

5 Please note that we are installing a new computer system. Under the new system reference numbers will change. Interspeed's new reference number will be INTUK/000215. Please quote this in future correspondence.

2 Look at fax B again. Match each heading (a – e) with a part of the text (1 – 5).

a action

b closing apology

c extra note (not related to main topic)

d explanation

e main apology

Grammar: articles

3 Look at fax B and decide if these statements are true or false.

a *A* (or *an*) usually means 'one' and is used before singular nouns.

b The first time we mention something, we often use *a*; after that we usually use *the*.

c We do not usually use *a* or *the* before names of countries and companies.

d We do not usually use *a* or *the* before nouns that refer to general things.

e We use *the* before nouns that refer to specific things.

4 Add articles (*a, an* or *the*) to this paragraph if you think they are necessary.

> We are hoping to go to ..... Olivetti, in Italy and we would like to make ..... visit to the photocopier factory there. Our shop sells ..... office equipment from a number of manufacturers. ..... visit will show us how ..... photocopiers are made. We are also hoping to meet ..... Production Manager.

 p.93 **Grammar backup 11**

P h r a s e b o o k

Formal apologies

I am sorry there is a delay.
I apologise for the mistake.
Please accept our apologies.
I hope you will accept our apologies.
I am afraid we cannot deliver tomorrow.
The reason for the delay is a missing component.
We will send it immediately.
Once again, I apologise for the inconvenience.

Writing faxes

5 Write an answer to the fax below. Use the expressions in the Phrasebook and organise the text of your fax like this:

1 main apology
2 explanation
3 action
4 closing apology

FROM AUTOBITS   0123467 765843   P . 1

FAX

To: Nash Computer Components Ltd.
From: J. Taylor, Autobits Ltd.
Date: August 21 1997   **Pages: 1**
Re: Our order no. 58317 (Dated July 20 1997)

The above order arrived yesterday but one of the components was incorrect. We ordered a 2 gigabyte disk drive and received a 1 gigabyte disk drive. Please let me know as soon as possible what arrangements you can make to correct the situation.

Word file Unit 11

LETTERS / MEMOS / FAXES	PERSONAL QUALITIES	
Best wishes	calm	convenient
cc	clear	courier
correspondence	confident	definitely
grateful for	confused	delay
look forward to	(un)cooperative	delivery
memo	(in)discreet	expect
memorandum	hostile	explanation
Re	nervous	including
reference number	relaxed	inconvenience
Regards		inform
subject	**OTHER**	install
Yours faithfully	apologise	probably
	apology	project
TELEPHONE	beyond our	reason
hang on	control	solution
hold on	certainly	

Grammar *backup 11*

will

Practice

1 Complete these sentences using *will* and the verb in brackets.

a Her plane will arrive at three o'clock in the morning. (arrive)
b The meeting ..... before dinner. (end)
c What time ..... the concert .....? (start)
d There ..... not ..... an office party this year. (be)
e Do you think they .....? (come)

2 In two of these sentences, *shall* is much better than *will*. Which two sentences?

a Will I order a pizza?
b Will they come?
c Will he work late tonight?
d Will we go to the cinema?
e Will you earn more in your new job?

3 Rewrite these sentences using short forms.

a I will not go to France.
   I won't go to France.
b I'm sure they will come.
c Do you think she will be good at the job?
d We will not get to the airport in time for our flight.

4 Translation

Write these sentences in your own language.

a He'll probably leave early.
b I'll catch the next train.
c Won't she find it difficult?
d Shall I order a taxi?
e He definitely won't like it.

Reference

We use **will** to:
• state facts about the future

EXAMPLES: *He **will** be here at 6.00 p.m.*
*The train **will** be late.*

• make predictions

EXAMPLE: *I think it **will** rain tomorrow.*

• express decisions

EXAMPLE: *I'**ll** have a pizza.*

• make requests

EXAMPLE: ***Will** you try to come?*

Shall is used in place of **will** for suggestions and offers with **I** and **we**.

EXAMPLE: ***Shall** I cook this evening?*

Statements

Will stays the same with all subjects. It is followed by an infinitive.

I/You/He/She It/We/They	will (not) won't	come.

Questions

Shall/Will	I/we	come?
Will	you/he/she it/they	come?

Short forms

Will is often shortened to **'ll** in speech and informal writing.

EXAMPLE: *I'**ll** see you later.*

Will not is often reduced to **won't** in speech and informal writing.

EXAMPLE: *She **won't** be there.*

Articles

Practice

1 *a* or *an*?

a *a* fax
b ..... meeting
c ..... answerphone
d ..... typewriter
e ..... Olivetti computer
f ..... hotel
g ..... airline
h ..... company
i ..... employer
j ..... international flight

2 Complete these with *a* or *some*.

a We've got *some* visitors.
b She's brought ..... parcel.
c There are ..... cold drinks in the fridge.
d Would you like ..... cup of tea?
e Can you order ..... sugar?

3 Complete the dialogue with *a, an, the* or no article.

A: I went to see (a) *a* great film last night.
B: Did you? Which one?
A: Well, (b)..... film was called *The Mosquito Coast*.
B: Oh yes, I've seen that – it's quite old, isn't it? Who's in it?
A: Well, (c)..... main actor is Harrison Ford.
B: That's right. It's about (d)..... man who takes his family and leaves (e)..... United States. They go to start (f)..... new life in another country, away from (g)..... cities, (h)..... people, and (i)..... modern life.
A: Yes, that's right.
B: Doesn't he go to (j)..... Brazil or (k)..... Paraguay?
A: I'm not sure exactly.
B: Where did you see it?
A: At (l)..... cinema near (m)..... station. You know – the Plaza.

4 Translation

Write this paragraph in your own language.

Five years ago I had a job in France. I sold educational books. Some people are good at selling. I wasn't. I found the job difficult. I didn't sell much but I learnt a lot of French.

Reference

It is a good idea to read about **a / some / any** again. See page 28.

Articles **a, an** and **the** and words like **some** and **any** come before nouns.

A / an

We use **a** (before a consonant) or **an** (before a vowel) to mean 'one'. We use them only with singular, countable nouns. We do not use them before plural and uncountable nouns.

EXAMPLE: *There was **a** bag on the table.*

We also use **a** when we refer to something for the first time.

EXAMPLE: *We've got **a** new house. It's not far from here.*

The

We use **the** when we refer to something a second time.

EXAMPLE: *I had **a** suitcase and **a** bag but I lost **the** bag.*

We also use **the** when we refer to an object that the hearer knows.

EXAMPLES: *I've been to **the** hotel.*
*He's cleaning **the** office.*

No article

We often use no article when we refer to things in general.

EXAMPLE: *She loves **cats**.*
*They have thousands of **books**.*

We also use no article when we refer to an uncountable noun generally or for the first time.

EXAMPLE: *It's made of **leather**.*

No article is used before most names of countries, towns and companies.

EXAMPLES: ***Recife** is in **Brazil**.*
***Olivetti** is in **Ivrea**.*

Note

For some countries we use **the**.

EXAMPLES: ***the** USA, **the** Philippines, **the** Netherlands*

Personal development

12

Action A Future plans

- Read about arrangements
- Discuss plans
- Vocabulary:
  - bookings
  - travel plans
- Grammar:
  going to

Reading: making arrangements

These faxes were both sent to ELEA, Olivetti's training centre in Italy.

A

olivetti
Telefax
Date: 9 February 1995
Number of pages (including cover sheet): 1

Olivetti North America
Product Marketing
22425 E. Appleway Ave.
Liberty Lake, WA 99019-9534
Telephone: (309) 927-5600

To: Elea Course Secretary   Fax No. 125 424553
From: Barbara Chassot/Admin. Asst. ONA   Fax No. (509) 927-5134

Subject: SNX 200 (Lark) Course

Please register the following person from Olivetti North America for the *SNX 200 (Lark) Course* scheduled from February 28th–March 3rd.

Attendee: Norm Carpenter/Olivetti North America
             Tel: 509/927-5650 Fax: 509/927-5718

Please send via fax, *confirmation of registration, course price/payment procedure.*
If you have any questions, please contact me at (509) 927-5134. Thank you in advance for your assistance.

Sincerely,

Barbara Chassot

B

olivetti
Telefax

Head Office
110 Silverwater Road
Silverwater NSW 2141
Australia

data
date 03/02/95

Pagine n• (compreso la presenta)
Number of pages (including cover sheet) 1

To: Antonella Faccin Fax no: 125-424.553

Divisione Informatica e Tecnologie

From: Margaret Mason Fax no: 61-2-745 3390

In case of bad transmission please telephone 61-2-741 6123

We confirm the attendance of Bob McGuirk for the following course:
SST 6715 of 6/2/95
PRP 600P of 13/2/95
His flight details are as follows:
Sunday 5 February arrival at Turin airport on flight BA580 at
11.00 from London.
Departure Saturday 18 February from Turin airport on flight BA581
at 18.30.
Would you please arrange transport to and from the airport and
also accommodation. Please advise the driver which hotel Mr
McGuirk is booked into.
Thank you for your assistance.
Kind regards,

Margaret Mason
Margaret Mason

---

1 Answer these questions about each fax.

a Which country is the fax from?
b Who is it from?
c Who is it addressed to?
d When was it sent?

2 Which fax:

a gives travel information?
b asks for information about a course?
c reserves a place on a course?
d is the second fax on this subject?
e asks for a reply?

3 What is the ELEA course secretary going to do for Mr Carpenter and Mr McGuirk, do you think?

4 Read the faxes again. Use words from the faxes to complete this chart.

verb	meaning	noun
register	put a person's name on a list	.....
.....	say that something is certain	confirmation
pay	.....	....
assist	help	.....
attend	be present at an event	.....
arrive	.....	.....
depart	leave	.....
.....	make plans for something	arrangement
....	reserve	booking

Grammar: *going to*

5 Look at the questions and statements.

Is the ELEA secretary going to register Norm Carpenter?
Yes she is.

She is going to book a hotel room for Bob McGuirk.
She is not going to book his meals.

a Which verb do we use before *going to*?

b What form of the verb follows *going to*?

6 Make questions and statements using *going to*.

a ELEA trainers / teach Mr Carpenter.
ELEA trainers are going to teach Mr Carpenter.

b you / contact Mr Chassot?

c Mr McGuirk / not / fly from Australia.

d Ms Mason / speak to the driver?

7 Answer questions about the ELEA secretary's plans. Give short answers.

a Is she going to register Mr Carpenter for a course?

b Is she going to send a letter to the United States?

c Is she going to write to Barbara Chassot?

8 Look at these sentences about Ms Faccin's plans. Are they true or false?

a She is going to register Bob McGuirk for two courses.

b She is going to buy plane tickets for him.

c She is not going to send a car to the airport for Mr McGuirk.

d She is not going to meet him at the airport.

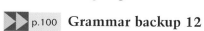 p.100 **Grammar backup 12**

Speaking: talking about plans

9 Work in pairs. Ask about your partner's plans for the future. Use these expressions to help you.

a after this class

b on Saturday evening

c next summer

d when you leave your present job

e in your old age

> EXAMPLE: *What are you going to do after this class?*
> *I'm going to have a cup of coffee.*

Tell the class about your partner's plans.

Phrasebook

Asking about plans

What are you going to do?
What's he going to do?
Where are they going to go?
When's the next meeting **going to be?**
How's she going to travel?

Writing about future plans

10 You are a course secretary. Read these fax extracts. What are you going to do? Write six sentences.

> EXAMPLE: *I am going to register Ms Scott on the July course.*

A

With reference to your fax of May 5th, please register Ms Scott on the July course and invoice us for the cost. Would you also arrange hotel accommodation for seven nights?

Thank you.

B

Re: Course TEC4

I regret that Mr Bedouelle cannot now attend the course as his wife is very ill. Please return his deposit and cancel his hotel booking.
Thank you for your assistance.

Yours sincerely,

Sophie Lebrun

C

Subject: Spanish course (SC27)
We have arranged payment for Mrs Bell's classes by bank transfer to your account. Please let us know when it arrives.

Sincerely,

Jeremy Notts

Action **B** # The best advice

Reading and Speaking: problems and advice

1 Read letter A from a problem page in a magazine.
a Was Jenny happy with her job at first? Is she happy now?
b Look at these suggestions.
 • She should apply for jobs in other companies.
 • She should get another qualification in her free time.
 • She should give up secretarial work.
 • She should continue with her present job.
 • She should discuss the problem with her boss.
 What do you think? Which is the best advice?

2 Now read letter B, the reply from the magazine adviser. Does the writer give Jenny the same advice as you did? What are the differences?

A

I left school at sixteen and did a secretarial course. Then I joined this company. It was all right at first, but after eight years I'm still doing the same job and I'm really bored. When I apply for promotion, they say that I haven't got the right qualifications. I can transfer to another department, but secretarial tasks are the same in any department. I don't know what to do. What do you think? Should I leave? Should I give up secretarial work?

Jenny

B

Dear Jenny

When you started work, you were probably just interested in having a job. Now you are older and you want something more – a career. In any career these days you should continue to take training courses. There are a lot of opportunities for people with secretarial skills to move into new areas such as sales, marketing and management.
In my opinion, you should go to your local college or adult education centre. Find out about courses that are available. There are full-time and part-time courses and you can even do correspondence courses, working for a qualification at home.
No, you shouldn't leave. I think you should stay in your job. Why don't you ask your boss to advise you on the best course to help your promotion chances? Most companies are happy to provide financial help and give time off to staff who want to learn new skills that are useful to the company.
It is clear that your company values your secretarial skills – you have been there for eight years. Now you should try to show them that you are prepared to work hard to improve your chances of promotion.

Good luck!

Phrasebook

Giving advice

What should I do?
You should leave.
I think you should stay in your job.
Why don't you do a training course?
In my opinion, you should stay.

3 Look again at letter B.
a Find all the phrases which the writer uses to give advice.
b Ask your partner about a problem that he / she has. Give some advice. Use expressions from the Phrasebook.

Vocabulary: career moves

4 Find verbs in letter A to complete these phrases.

a *leave* school
b ..... a company
c ..... a job
d ..... promotion
e ..... a qualification
f ..... to a different department

5 Match each verb with a word or phrase in Exercise 4. Sometimes more than one answer is possible.

move   start   get   ask for   work for   qualify for

6 Find words in letter B to complete these explanations:

a If you do a ..... course, you have to stop work and attend a college every day.
b You can do a ..... course in the evenings, or you can arrange a day or two off work each week.
c If you do a ..... course, you can study at home in your free time and write to your teacher.

Listening to a telephone conversation

7 🔊 Listen to part of a telephone conversation. Answer these questions.

a What happened two years ago?
b Is Paul working now?
c What does he want to do?

8 What do you think these words and phrases mean?

a a computer programmer
b unemployed
c freelance work
d a proper job
e out of touch
f to retrain

Grammar: verb patterns

9 Look at these sentences from the conversation:

• *I want to get a proper job.*
• *I need to earn more.*
• *I'd like to stay in computing.*

a Which underlined verb has a different meaning from the other two?
b What word follows all three expressions?
c Which verb does not change if the sentence begins with *she*?
d What is the full form of *'d like*?

▶▶ p.101 **Grammar backup 12**

Speaking and Writing: wishes and needs

10 Work in pairs. Look at the picture.

a Ask and answer questions about the things this woman <u>would like</u> to do and <u>needs</u> to do.

EXAMPLE: *What do you think she'd like to do?*
She'd like to take a long holiday, but she needs to pay her bills.

wishes   needs

b Now imagine you are the woman. Decide what you are going to do. Answer your partner's questions about your plans.

EXAMPLE: *What are you going to do?*
I'm going to pay my bills and take a short holiday.

Phrasebook

Asking about wishes and needs

What would you like to do?
Where do you want to work?
How much do you need to earn?

---

11 Write sentences explaining what you would like to do when you finish this English course. Then write what you need to do. Finally, write what you are in fact going to do, if you have any plans.

Action C

Language training

- Explain language learning needs
- Complete a form
- Discuss problems and solutions
- Grammar:
  too and *(not) enough*

Discussion: secretarial responsibilities

1   Imagine you are a secretary in an international company like Olivetti. Make a list of the tasks you will probably do in English as part of your job.

Listening to an interview

2   Liana Marsan runs foreign language courses at ELEA. These courses are for Olivetti staff, and also for employees of other companies. What important reason does she give for learning:

a   English?
b   other languages?

Writing and Speaking: completing a form

3   When students come to ELEA for an English course, they complete a questionnaire. This helps them to be clear about their needs. Complete this questionnaire to show your own needs in English. If you are not sure, imagine a job that you would like to have.

Name: ....

1   Do you use English now for your work or studies? ....
Do you hope to use it in the future? ....

2   Number these in order of their importance for you:
Speaking ....   Understanding speech ....
Writing ....   Reading ....

3   How many hours a week do you / will you use English in your work or studies? ....

4   Do you / will you have contact with native speakers of English? ....

5   Give details of your previous study of English.
....
....

6   Give details of visits to English-speaking countries.
....
....

7   What areas of English are a particular problem for you?
....
....

8   What skills would you like to have at the end of the course?
....
....

Talking point

WHY ARE WE LEARNING ENGLISH? IF PEOPLE WANT TO CONTACT ME, THEY SHOULD LEARN MY LANGUAGE.

What do *you* think?

4   **Look at your partner's form and ask for more information.**

EXAMPLE: *Why is understanding speech more important for you than speaking?*

Listening: English for secretaries

5 🔊 **Liana is talking about telephone conversations. Listen.**

a Why are these conversations difficult?
b What is Liana's advice to secretaries?

Discussion: problems and solutions

6 **Read these comments about telephone calls.**

a Which comments are about problems? Which are about solutions?
b Do you have these problems? What are your solutions?

> I TAKE NOTES WHILE I LISTEN. THEN AT THE END OF THE CONVERSATION I READ THE NOTES TO THE CALLER.

A

> TELEPHONE CALLS ARE VERY FRIGHTENING. SOME PEOPLE SPEAK TOO FAST AND I DON'T KNOW HOW TO STOP THEM.

B

> PEOPLE TELEPHONE FROM ALL OVER THE WORLD AND I DON'T ALWAYS UNDERSTAND THEIR ACCENTS.

C

> MY TECHNICAL ENGLISH IS NOT GOOD ENOUGH FOR DISCUSSIONS WITH ENGINEERS AND TECHNICIANS.

D

> MY ENGLISH IS ONLY GOOD ENOUGH TO TAKE SHORT MESSAGES. IF THE MESSAGE IS A LONG ONE, I ASK THEM TO SEND A FAX.

E

Grammar: *too* and *(not) enough*

7 **Read what some secretaries said.**

a Some people speak very quickly.
b Some people speak too quickly.
c My English is good.
d My English is good enough.
e My English is not good enough.

Which two secretaries definitely have a problem?

8 **Look back at the sentences in Exercise 7. Do *too* and *(not) enough* come before or after adjectives and adverbs?**

9 **Imagine you are the person in each of the pictures below. Make a statement with *too* or *(not) enough*.**

EXAMPLE: *I can't reach that file. It's too high. / I'm not tall enough:*

▶▶ p.101 **Grammar backup 12**

Writing about your language skills

10 Write a paragraph about your present and / or future use of English. Include information about:

- your level and use of English now.
- jobs you are going to do.
- skills you would like to have.
- areas that you need to improve.
- ways of solving your problems in English.

Word file Unit 12

COURSES	WORK	OTHER
attend	apply (for)	advise
attendance	freelance	need
confirmation	join	should
correspondence	promotion	want
course	retrain	would like
payment		
register	**ARRANGEMENTS**	
registration	assist	
training course	assistance	
	cooperation	

going to

Practice

1 **A friend is visiting James at work. It is his first visit to the company. Complete his questions with *going to* and the verbs in brackets.**

F: So this is your office. It's quite small, isn't it?

J: Yes, it is. In fact we've decided to move. The company is too big for these offices now.

F: I agree. When (a) *are you going to move?* (move)

J: In the summer, when most of our clients are on holiday.

F: (b)..... in this area? (stay)

J: Yes, I like being in the town centre.

F: (c)..... new furniture? (buy)

J: No, I don't think so. These desks are fine.

F: How (d)..... your clients ..... you? (find)

J: We're going to put advertisements in the newspapers.

F: (e)..... a party? (have)

J: I'm not sure, but we'll invite you if we do!

2 **Give short answers in response to these questions.**

a Are you going to complete this English course?
Yes, I am.

b Are you and your family going to have a holiday this summer?

c Is your country's football team going to play a match this weekend?

d Are all the people in your class going to work for foreign companies after this course?

3 **Make these sentences negative.**

a We're going to work hard.
We aren't going to work hard.

b She's going to ask for promotion.

c I'm going to transfer to another department.

d They're going to have a Christmas dance.

e You're going to earn more next year.

4 **Translation**

Write these sentences in your own language.

a What are you going to do after work?

b Is he going to go to the cinema?

c I'm going to prepare for the meeting.

d We aren't going to be there.

Reference

We use **going to** when we talk about plans or intentions for the future.

EXAMPLE: *I'm **going to** visit my parents after work.*

Going to is used with the verb **to be** and it is followed by an infinitive.

I am You are He is She is It is We are They are	going to	help.

• We add **not** to make a negative form.

EXAMPLES: *I am **not going to** help.*
*She **isn't / is not going to** play.*

• We change the position of the subject and the **be** auxiliary to make a question.

EXAMPLES: ***Are we going to** win?*
*Why **is he going to** leave?*

• We use **am / are / is** in short answers.

EXAMPLE: *Are you going to come?*
*Yes, I **am**.*

SO WHAT ARE YOU GOING TO BRING HOME NEXT?

too / (not) enough

Practice

1 Jane and Simon are looking for a quiet, two-week holiday in the sun in May. They don't like long flights and they can't spend more than £500.

Why is the holiday in the advertisement not a good one for them? Use these adjectives and *too / not enough* to write five sentences.

> expensive   long   far   quiet   late   hot

EXAMPLE: *It's too expensive.*

2 The speaker is suggesting tasks for a new project team. Disagree with the suggestions, using the adverbs in brackets.

a Penny can write our objectives. (clearly)
She won't write them clearly enough.
b Tania can do research. (carefully)
c Ron can talk to clients. (politely)
d I can type reports. (fast)
e Pat can translate them into German. (accurately)
f Tim can design advertisements. (professionally)
g Brenda can sell the new products. (cheaply)

3 Translation
Write these sentences in your own language

a This exercise is too difficult.
b My English is not good enough.
c They pay us well enough.

PASTEN ISLAND

A popular island resort with luxury hotels, discos, shopping and good sports facilities.
Average temperatures 12°C (winter), 22°C (summer). Only 9 hours flying time from Heathrow. 7 or 10-day holidays from £350 per person, including all meals.

Holiday periods 2.6 – 28.9, 17.12 – 30.1

Reference

We use **too** and (**not**) **enough** to talk about a problem.
EXAMPLES: *She's **too** advanced for this class.*
*He is**n't** strong **enough** to carry those boxes.*

Too is followed by an adjective or an adverb.
EXAMPLES: *I'm **too cold**.*
*You're driving **too quickly**.*

An adjective or an adverb comes between a negative verb and **enough**.
EXAMPLES: *I'm **not warm enough**.*
*You **aren't driving slowly enough**.*

Enough is also used with a positive meaning when the situation is satisfactory.
EXAMPLE: *I'm warm **enough**.*

Verb patterns: *should, would like, want, need*

Practice

1 **Add *to* if it is necessary.**
A: Would you like (a) *to* come into my office?
B: Certainly. Do I need (b)..... bring anything?
A: We need (c)..... have the Tenby report. I think we should (d)..... look at it again.
B: I see. Do you want (e)..... make some changes?
A: I'm not sure. We'll see.
B: Should I (f)..... bring the computer disk?
A: No, I only want (g)..... see the paper document.

2 Translation
Write these sentences in your own language.

a He should practise his English.
b I want to join the company.

Reference

Should, **would like**, **want** and **need** are all followed by the infinitive form of another verb.
Should is followed by an infinitive without *to*.
EXAMPLE: *You **should change** jobs.*

Would like, **want** and **need** are often followed by *to* + infinitive.
EXAMPLES: *I'**d like to meet** her.*
*She **wants to meet** you.*
*We **need to talk**.*

They are also followed by a noun.
EXAMPLES: *I'**d like a better job**.*
*She **wants a copy** of your report.*
*We **need help**.*

Gillian Peters is Lorna Davies' secretary. When she starts work in the morning her first job is to listen to the messages on the answerphone.

1 🔊 **Listen to all the messages.**

a Which messages need:
  • urgent action?   • non-urgent action?   • no action?

b Which messages does Gillian make these notes about?

TELEPHONE MESSAGE

CALLER: Lorna
FOR:

MESSAGE/ACTION

Fax Sally Thomas.
Change meeting from 10.30 to 11.30

☐ TELEPHONED   ☐ WILL RING BACK
                        ☐ WOULD LIKE TO SEE YOU
                        ☐ URGENT

TELEPHONE MESSAGE

CALLER: RJ Deliveries
FOR:

MESSAGE/ACTION

Fax new address to RJ Deliveries
Fax no. 387 4002

☐ TELEPHONED   ☐ WILL RING BACK
☐ PLEASE RING   ☐ WOULD LIKE TO SEE YOU
☐ RETURNED YOUR CALL   ☐ URGENT

2 🔊 **Listen to messages A and B again. Complete message forms like the forms above.**

3   Work in pairs and arrange a meeting.
   A: Turn to page 139.
   B: You are Gillian Peters. Look at Lorna Davies'
   diary below. Call David Long's secretary and
   confirm the time of the meeting.

11 June	Monday
10.30 Sally Thomas	
Afternoon – Finance meeting. Rm 201	

12 June	Tuesday
9. 00 – 11.00 interviews. Board room	
3.00 – 6.00 p.m. interviews. Rm 205	

13 June	Wednesday
interviews all morning. Board room	
3.00 p.m. Anna Grodzinski	

14 June	Thursday
Lunch 12.00 – 2.00 with GE	
2.30 – 5.00 Finance meeting. Rm 201	

15 June	Friday
2.00 – 3.30 interviews. Board room	

**4   ▣ Listen to message C. Make notes. Then
   complete this fax to Sally Thomas.**

FAX TRANSMISSION

To: Sally Thomas

From: Lorna Davies' secretary

Date: Tuesday June 12th

I'm afraid Ms Davies ....
....

5   ▣ Listen to messages D, E and F.
a   Write messages if they are necessary.
b   Write a short letter to send with an application
    form.

6   ▣ Listen to messages G and H.
a   Write the message for G.
b   Write a fax to RJ Deliveries. Use information from
    your boss's business card.

DT Technology

Lorna Davies

Public Relations Manager

5th floor, Arundel House
New Oxford Street
London W1 4SD

Tel: 0171 392 0569
Fax: 0171 392 0570

7   Work in pairs and leave answerphone messages.

   A: Leave messages for situations a – c below.
   B: Call back and leave an answerphone message
      in reply. Make up any information you need.

a   You want to know what time the company's
    offices are open on Saturdays.
b   You would like to know when Mr Daniels is
    coming back from his holiday.
c   You want to know what time the reception on
    June 16th begins.

   B: Leave messages for situations d – f below.
   A: Call back and leave an answerphone message
      in reply. Make up any information you need.

d   You want to change a meeting with Ms Vincent
    from Monday morning to Tuesday morning. You
    are available any time on Tuesday morning.
e   You cannot find an invoice that a company has
    sent you. Call them and ask for the invoice
    number.
f   Your boss went to a meeting yesterday and thinks
    she left a bag there. You want to know if someone
    found it.

Facts and figures

13

Action **A** ## International Herald Tribune

- Understand statistics
- Find out about collecting statistics
- Grammar:
  present perfect with *just*, *yet* and *already*

Discussion: international newspapers

1 How many international newspapers can you name? How often do they appear? What languages are they in? Do you read any of them?

Listening: understanding statistics

2 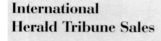 Listen. An employee of the International Herald Tribune is talking about sales of the newspaper. Complete the chart with the missing information.

International Herald Tribune Sales

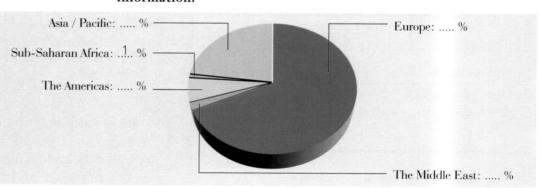

Asia / Pacific: ..... %
Sub-Saharan Africa: ..1.. %
The Americas: ..... %
Europe: ..... %
The Middle East: ..... %

3 Use information from the chart to finish these sentences.

a The majority of sales are in Europe.
b Almost a quarter of sales are in ..... .
c Almost three-quarters of sales are in ..... .
d Two very small areas for sales are ..... and ..... .
e ..... represent a fairly small percentage of sales.

Reading: collecting statistics

4 Read about Yveline Cochennec and answer these questions.

a Where does Yveline Cochennec work?
b Where does she collect sales figures from?
c Where does she send them? How often?

Yveline Cochennec works in the Marketing Department of the International Herald Tribune (IHT) in Paris. One part of her job is to collect useful information and statistics about the newspaper and its readers. The paper uses this information to persuade companies to buy advertising space. She collects the sales figures that come in from the IHT offices all over the world and sends the information to a company called OJD. OJD checks the figures and publishes the official sales of IHT and thousands of other newspapers and magazines. The chart above shows one year's official sales statistics.

'We haven't received the official figures for this year yet. I've already sent OJD the sales figures for the first three quarters of the year and I've just collected the figures for the fourth quarter.'

Vocabulary: statistics research

5 **Find these words in the text in Exercise 4.**

marketing   collect   statistics   figures
check   quarter

Match each word with an explanation below.

a three months of the year (e.g. January–March)
b to bring together from different places
c numbers
d information in the form of numbers
e look carefully at something
f a business activity that involves advertising and selling

Grammar: present perfect with *just, yet* and *already*

6 **Look at these sentences from the text and answer questions about them.**

a *We haven't received the official figures for this year yet.*

  • Has IHT got the official figures?
  • Are the figures going to come?

b *I've already sent OJD the sales figures ...*

  • Has OJD got the sales figures?
  • Do we know when Yveline sent them?

c *I've just collected the figures ...*

  • Has Yveline got these figures?
  • Did she collect them a long time ago?
  • Do we know exactly when she collected them?

7 **Find the verbs in sentences a – c above. How is the present perfect formed?**

8 **Make sentences using the present perfect and *just, yet* or *already*. Use the verbs in brackets.**

EXAMPLES: *I'm taking my driving test next week. (pass)*
I haven't passed my driving test yet.

a Mr Jackson isn't here, but I expect him soon. (arrive)
b I posted the letter five minutes ago. (post)
c We discussed the plans yesterday. We don't need to talk about them again. (discuss)
d The floor's wet. The cleaner washed it. (wash)

▶▶ p.110   **Grammar backup 13**

Speaking: questions and answers

9 ***Yet* is common in present perfect questions. Work in pairs. Look at the picture. Ask and answer questions about:**

  • the office staff   • the manager
  • the cleaner   • the rubbish collectors

EXAMPLE: *Has the security guard started work yet?*
Yes, he has.

Talking point

STATISTICS ARE JUST OFFICIAL LIES.

What do *you* think?

Action B # Collecting information

- Understand a questionnaire
- Read a survey
- Write a survey report
- Grammar:
  past simple and present
  perfect

Discussion: a reader survey

1 **Every few years a questionnaire is sent to readers of the International Herald Tribune. Then a reader survey is produced.**

a Answer the questions from the questionnaire on the left with information about yourself.

b Why do you think the newspaper is interested in this information?

How many languages do you have at least a knowledge of, apart from your mother tongue?

One ☐   Four ☐   ☐
Two ☐   Five ☐   ☐
Three ☐ Six or more ☐ ☐

Are you currently:

Working full/part-time ☐
Student ☐
Retired ☐

What is your job title or position?

Owner/Partner ☐
Chairman/President ☐
Managing Director ☐
General Manager ☐
Vice President ☐
Other Director ☐
Consultant ☐
Other Senior Management ☐
Middle Management ☐
Senior Government Officer / ☐
Politician / Diplomat ☐
Professional (Education, Legal, Medical) ☐
Other ☐

Approximately how many nights have you spent in hotels in the last 12 months?

1-7 ☐   8-14 ☐   15-29 ☐   30-49 ☐
50-74 ☐   75-99 ☐   100+ ☐

How often do you read the IHT?

5-6 days a week ☐
3-4 days a week ☐
1-2 days a week ☐

SUMMARY OF FINDINGS

Here is a brief introduction to the readers of the International Herald Tribune – the World's Daily Newspaper:

63% of readers live in Europe, 19% in Asia and 14% in the USA. 92% have been educated to degree level, and 40% speak at least three languages.

82% of those in commerce or industry are senior managers: this represents 211,000 readers daily.

94% – that is 430,000 readers – have flown internationally during the past year. In fact, the IHT is read each day by an audience who makes over 5 million international air trips annually.

IHT readers spend an average of 36 nights a year in hotels, which means that the newspaper's readership represents an annual total of over 16 million hotel nights.

The average annual household income of the IHT reader is US$ 164,000, which means that every day, the IHT is read by an audience who collectively earns an average annual household income of more than US$ 31 billion.

The average value of each reader's household investments is US$ 957,000. Each day, the newspaper is read by a group with collective household investments of over US$ 182 billion.

Each day the International Herald Tribune is read by almost half a million internationally-minded, mobile, affluent, well-educated and successful men and women in over 180 countries around the world.

Reading and Writing: a survey summary

2 **Companies that want to advertise in the IHT read the Reader Survey. Read the Summary of Findings above.**

a Are all the questions on the left answered in the Summary? Which ones are not?

b Choose two other pieces of information in the Summary. Write the questions.

Vocabulary: market information

3 Find these phrases in the Summary. Guess their meaning. Use a dictionary to check your answers.

- brief introduction
- senior managers
- air trips
- an average of
- annual total
- household income
- household investments

Reading a survey report

4 Look at this extract from a Reader Survey and a report based on the extract.

)TEL NIGHTS *Approximately how many nights have you spent in hotels in the last 12 months?*

ders of the IHT
d over 16
ion nights in
ds a year.

	Worldwide
1+ nights	94%
8+ nights	84%
15+ nights	69%
30+ nights	45%
50+ nights	25%
75+ nights	14%
100 or more nights	9%
Average number of nights	36

In the last 12 months IHT readers have stayed in hotels for an average of 36 nights. Nine per cent have spent at least 100 nights away from home, 14 per cent have been away for 75 nights or more and 25 per cent have used hotels for a minimum of 50 nights. 94 per cent of readers have stayed in hotels for at least one night. In total, IHT readers have spent over 16 million nights in hotels in the last 12 months.

a Where does the writer give a summary of the results?
b Find other phrases that mean *to stay in hotels* in the report. Why does the writer use different phrases do you think?
c Which of these phrases has a different meaning from the others?
- at least 50 nights
- 50 nights or more
- over 50 nights
- a minimum of 50 nights

Grammar: past simple and present perfect

5 Look again at the texts in Exercise 4.

a Which tense is used in the survey question?
b Which tense is used in the report?
c What is the correct tense for a report that begins 'Last year ...' ?

▶▶ p.111 **Grammar backup 13**

Writing a survey report

6 Look at two more extracts from the same Reader Survey. Write two short reports similar to the report in Exercise 4.

FREQUENCY OF AIR TRAVEL *Approximately how many international air trips have you made in the last 12 months?*

IHT readers collectively take over 5 million international air trips a year

	Worldwide
Any trip	94%
3+ trips	77%
6+ trips	54%
11+ trips	34%
20+ trips	19%
35 or more trips	8%
Average number of air trips	12

SEX AND AGE *Are you ...*

	Worldwide
Male	79%
Female	21%
Under 25	4%
25-34	21%
35-44	24%
45-54	25%
55-64	16%
65+	10%
Average age	45

Action C # Presenting information

- Talk about possibilities
- Present information
- Vocabulary:
  - newspapers and magazines
  - numbers and amounts

Vocabulary: newspapers and magazines

1 Look at these words. You can use them to talk about newspapers and magazines.

> daily   weekly   monthly   national   local   international

Which words can you use to describe the newspapers and magazines below, do you think?

2 Think about newspapers and magazines in your country. Name:

a   a local daily newspaper.
b   a monthly international magazine.
c   a national weekly magazine.
d   a national daily newspaper.
e   a weekly local newspaper.
f   a national monthly magazine.

Listening and Speaking: talking about possibilities

3 🔊 Look at the newspaper titles from around the world on the left.
Listen and read. Two people are trying to guess where newspaper A is from.

Man: What language is this? It looks like Spanish.
Woman: Oh yes. It's definitely Spanish. So it could be from Spain.
Man: Yes. But it might be from another country, like Argentina, for example.
Woman: Oh, yes. Or Chile, or Ecuador.

4 **Work in pairs. Try to guess where the other newspapers are from. Use expressions from the Phrasebook.**

Phrasebook

Possibilities

It **looks like** Spanish.
He **looks like** a footballer.
She **could be** Brazilian.
I think he's **probably** older than me.

Reading and Listening: numbers and amounts

5 **Match these numbers with numbers in the newspaper extracts below.**

a 1/2
b 2/3
c seventy-three point eight
d one – nil

e fifteen per cent
f six-oh
g six point two eight
h nought point two

A

For an information pack, call the number below:

0345 60 90 60

B

15% Off Home & Motor Insurance

British women can expect to live, on average, for 79.1 years, and men for 73.8 years.

C

The shock 1 – 0 defeat against Azerbaijan was the biggest upset in Swiss football history.

D

Nearly half of all parents say primary school teachers give them little or no information on how to help with their children's education. Two-thirds do not understand what their children are learning.

E

Around Britain

	Sun (hours)
Aberdeen	3.6
Belfast	0.2
Birmingham	2.9

F

Wall Street

New York: The Dow Jones industrial average index rose 6.28 points to close at 5,894.74.

G

6 🔊 **Listen. Match the numbers you hear with the numbers below.**

- 65%
- 0.13
- 13%
- 7/12

- 28.4
- 1/3
- 82.4
- 7.12

Listen again and practise saying the numbers.

Speaking and Writing: collecting and presenting information

7 **Work in pairs.**

a Decide what information you want to collect about other people's reading habits. Write questions to ask.

EXAMPLE: *How many magazines have you read in the last month?*

b Interview as many people as you can. Note their answers.

c Write a report about your results.

EXAMPLE: *Ten per cent of the group never read magazines, but fifty per cent have read three or more in the last month.*

Word file   Unit 13

SURVEYS	nought	national
collect	per cent	weekly
findings	point two five	
sales figures	two-fifths	**OTHER**
statistics	two point eight	annual
summary		average
survey	**NEWSPAPERS/**	brief
	MAGAZINES	household
NUMBERS	daily	income
a half	international	investment
a third	local	senior
nil	monthly	

Present perfect with *just, yet* and *already*

Practice

1 Choose the correct position for the words in brackets.

a Ms Devlin ..... hasn't arrived ..✓.. . (yet)
b Have the painters ..... finished .....? (yet)
c Oh no! The post ..... has ..... gone. (already)
d Have you ..... had ..... lunch? (just)
e I've ..... read ..... the report. (already)
f We haven't received ..... the information ..... . (yet)
g The cleaners ..... have ..... finished. (already)
h Has ..... the parcel arrived .....? (yet)
i You've ..... missed her ..... . (just)
j I've sent ..... the sales information ..... . (already)

2 Make sentences or questions using the present perfect with *just, already* or *yet*.

a You are waiting for a parcel that is late. Ask if it has come.
   Has the parcel come yet?
b Your friend offers you a cup of tea. Say no. You had one a few minutes ago.
c Your boss reminds you to finish a report. You are surprised – you finished it yesterday. Tell her.
d Your boss tells you to send the sales figures to head office. Unfortunately they are not ready. You plan to do them today. Tell him.
e Your friend tells you that the boss is away on a business trip. But you saw the boss five minutes ago in reception. Tell her.

3 Translation
   Write these sentences in your own language.

a I've seen him.
b I've already seen him.
c I've just seen him.
d I haven't seen him yet.

Reference

We use the present perfect when we are interested in the present effects of something that happened in the past. It is not clear, or important, exactly when it happened.

EXAMPLE: *He's left the company.*
             (So he is not at the company now.)

The present perfect is formed with **have / has** + past participle. (See page 119 for past participles of irregular verbs.)

Statements

I/You/We/They	have(n't) have (not)	left.
He/She/It	has(n't) has (not)	

Questions

Have	I/you/we/they	left?
Has	he/she/it	

Short answers

Yes, No,	I/you/we/they	have. haven't / have not.
Yes, No,	he/she/it	has. hasn't / has not.

Already means before now, perhaps earlier than people expected.

EXAMPLE: *He has **already** left.*

Just means a short time before now.

EXAMPLE: *They have **just** gone.*

Yet is used to ask if something has happened (because you are expecting it to happen). It is also used in negative statements.

EXAMPLES: ***Have** they **come yet?***
             *It **hasn't arrived yet.***

Usual positions for **just, already** and **yet** are:

I've	(just) (already)	done it	(already)	.

I haven't		done it	(yet)	.

Have you	(just) (already)	done it	(already) (yet)	?

Past simple and present perfect

Practice

1 Past simple or present perfect? Choose the correct verb form.

I (a) left (left / have left) college in July last year and in the last few months I (b)..... (had / have had) three jobs. The first (c)..... (was / has been) a temporary job in a factory. I (d)..... (stayed / have stayed) there until October. Then I (e)..... (got / have got) a new job as a sales assistant in a shop. I (f)..... (didn't like / haven't liked) that and in January I (g)..... (began / have begun) working here at the hotel. I (h)..... (worked / have worked) on the reception desk since February and I enjoy it very much. I (i)..... (met / have met) a lot of nice people in the last few months and I think I (j)..... (found / have found) a job that I want to do for a long time.

2 Translation

Write these sentences in your own language.

a I started a new job yesterday.
b Did you enjoy your holiday last week?
c I haven't seen her today.
d All my life I have wanted to go to India.

HAS ARTHUR BEEN ON A NEW COMPUTER COURSE?

Reference

We use the past simple to refer to things that happened at a particular time in the past.

EXAMPLE:

She worked for the company	last year. last week. yesterday. in the 1980s. when she was sixteen. twenty years ago.

(She does not work for the company now.) Our interest is in the past and what happened then.

Compare this with the use of the present perfect.

EXAMPLES: She **has worked** here in the last few months.
(We do not know, or it is not important, exactly when.)

She **has been** here this morning.
(This is important because you are looking for her now, or because there is some effect of her visit. It is also possible that she is still in the building now.)

Regular verbs

The past simple and past participle forms are the same and end in **-ed.**
look — look**ed** — look**ed**
play — play**ed** — play**ed**

Irregular verbs

You need to learn the forms of these verbs separately. They do not end in -ed and the past simple form is often different from the past participle. (See page 119.)

Careers

14

Job histories

- Find out about a job history
- Vocabulary:
  jobs
- Grammar:
  present perfect with
  for and *since*

Discussion: success at work

1 **Read the statements below. Do you agree? Give your reasons.**

IN MY EXPERIENCE QUALIFICATIONS ARE NOT VERY IMPORTANT. PERSONALITY AND HARD WORK HELP YOU SUCCEED. **A**

TWENTY YEARS AGO YOU COULD FIND AN OFFICE JOB WITH SECONDARY SCHOOL QUALIFICATIONS. NOW YOU NEED A UNIVERSITY QUALIFICATION TO DO THE SAME JOB. **B**

DECIDE WHAT YOU WANT TO DO AND AIM FOR IT. DON'T ACCEPT ANYTHING LESS. **C**

YOU HAVE TO TAKE ANY JOB YOU CAN GET. YOU ONLY GET THE PERFECT JOB BY CHANCE. **D**

Listening and Reading: a job history

2   **Listen. Caroline Delon, a French woman, is talking about her career. Which of these jobs has Caroline done?**

- journalist
- secretary
- personal assistant
- waitress
- driver
- film editor
- translator
- tourist guide
- barmaid

3 **Listen and read. Put the list of Caroline's jobs in the right order.**

'I went to university and studied languages – English and Spanish – and business administration. When I left I had no idea what I wanted to do, but I knew the jobs I *didn't* want. You know: I never wanted a boring job in an office. I wanted to meet people, travel, use my languages. I took lots of temporary jobs, just to earn some money. I was a waitress, I served behind a bar ... er ... and I worked as a guide for a travel company. You know, showing tourists around Paris.

Then I got a job as a secretary with an advertising agency. I can't remember exactly how I got the job. I could type, but I think I knew someone who worked there and she introduced me to her boss – something like that. Anyway, one of the clients of the advertising agency was this film company, called Talking Pictures, and I started working for them. I stayed there for quite a long time – about 5 years – as the Personal Assistant to the Managing Director. I learned a lot about the film industry. I started to write about films for a magazine and now I work for the magazine full-time as a journalist.

It's strange really. I've worked for about twelve years now, since I left university, and have I ever had a real job interview? No, I haven't. In all that time I haven't had an interview! I've never sat down and decided I wanted to do a particular job. Life's not like that any more.'

4 **Read this information about Caroline. Is it true or false? Correct the false sentences.**

a Caroline always wanted to work in an office.
b Her mother introduced her to someone who ran an advertising agency.
c Talking Pictures is a film company.
d She met the people at Talking Pictures when she was at the advertising agency.
e She worked as a translator at the film company.
f She started in journalism by writing articles about business administration.
g She started her present job twelve years ago.
h She left university twelve years ago.
i She had a lot of interviews before she got her present job.

Grammar: present perfect with *for* and *since*

5 **Look at this extract from the interview. Notice the use of the present perfect.**

EXAMPLE: *'I've worked for about twelve years now, since I left university, and have I ever had a real job interview? No, I haven't. In all that time I haven't had an interview!'*

a Which word, *for* or *since*, is followed by:
• a point in time? • a period of time?

b Complete these expressions with *for* or *since*.

..... Saturday   ..... 8.30 a.m.
..... January 5th   ..... three days
..... five years   1995
..... two weeks   ..... two hours
..... I finished school

6 **Complete these sentences with the present perfect and *for* or *since*.**

a She *has worked* (work) there *since* 1990.
b '..... you ..... (see) him ..... lunchtime?'
'No, I ..... .'
c I ..... (not had) a pay increase ..... two years.
d They ..... (live) in Sweden ..... about ten years.
e '..... he ..... (speak) to you ..... last night?'
'Yes, he ....'
f We ..... (be) in this building ..... January.
g The company ..... (have) this contract ..... the last six months.

7 **Which of the structures below is used to talk about:**

a regular routines and present situations?
b future plans and intentions?
c actions and situations at a particular time in the past?
d situations that started in the past and are continuing now?
• present perfect   • past simple
• present simple   • *going to* + infinitive

▶▶ p.118 **Grammar backup 14**

Speaking: questions and answers

8 **Work in pairs. Ask for this information. Then ask and answer questions with *How long ...*?**

EXAMPLE: *Do you play any sport?*
Yes, I play tennis.
How long have you played tennis?
I've played tennis for about ten years.

• Have you got a job?
• Have you got a driving licence?
• Do you own a computer?
• Are you learning any languages?
• Do you live near here?
• Do you play a musical instrument?

Talking point

WHY SHOULD I WORK AT SCHOOL? THERE AREN'T ANY JOBS FOR SCHOOL-LEAVERS ANYWAY.

What do *you* think?

Action B # A curriculum vitae

- Read a CV
- Vocabulary:
  - qualifications
  - jobs and employment

Discussion: job applications

1 Work in pairs or groups. Discuss these questions.

a What do you need to send to an employer before a job interview?

b What information about you does an employer need to have?

> past jobs   details of qualifications   present job
> personal information   list of illnesses   foreign languages
> parents' jobs   copies of letters from previous employers
> marital status   hobbies   copy of driving licence
> plans for having children   age

CURRICULUM VITAE

Personal Information

Name: Rachel Tyson
Address: 44 Grange Road, Henley, OX20 2JE
Telephone: (01734) 299610
Age: 25   Date of Birth: 18th March 1972
Male/Female: Female

Educational Qualifications

Summer 1993: Diploma in French Studies. Sorbonne, Paris
1993: BA (Media Studies). Northern University
1990: A levels in English, Mathematics and Economics
1988: GCSE: English Language (A) English Literature (A)
Mathematics (A) Economics (A) French (B) History (B) Chemistry (C)
Biology (C) Drama (C) Spanish (C)

Career History

- Present position (since Oct 1995): Sales Manager, Playhouse Theatre, Cambridge
- August 1994 – September 1995: Marketing Assistant, Byron Books, Barcelona, Spain
- September 1993 – July 1994: Administrative Assistant, Marsh Advertising, London.

Skills

- fluent French
- conversational Spanish
- full driving licence

Hobbies and Interests

I enjoy travelling, music and sports. I play the violin and piano and I belong to a tennis and squash club. I also ski and I am learning to fly.

Referees

R.G. Jones, Director, Playhouse Theatre, Bridge Street, Cambridge CB1 2XL
J. Lluch, Marketing Manager, Byron Books, 85 Carrer Calabria, Barcelona

Reading a CV

2 Look at this curriculum vitae.

a Which information from your list in Exercise 1 does it contain? Does it contain any other information?

b Which short forms mean:
- a Bachelor of Arts degree from a university?
- the General Certificate of Secondary Education?

c Look at Rachel's school subjects. Write the subjects in two lists:
- science subjects: mathematics
- arts subjects: English Language

d Add other school subjects to your lists. Use a dictionary to help you.

e What does *referee* mean in this context? Someone who:
- is a past employer.
- controls some sports (e.g. football, boxing).
- can tell you about a person's character and skills.

Vocabulary: qualifications

3 Look at these British academic qualifications. Are qualifications similar in your country?

UNIVERSITY DEGREES

FIRST DEGREES:
BA (Bachelor of Arts) BSc (Bachelor of Science)

HIGHER DEGREES:
MA (Master of Arts) MSc (Master of Science)
PGCE (Postgraduate Certificate in Education)
MBA (Master of Business Administration)
MEd (Master of Education)
PhD (Doctor of Philosophy)

SECONDARY SCHOOL QUALIFICATIONS

Secondary school (at age 16): GCSEs, usually in six or more subjects.
Secondary school (at age 18): A levels, usually in three subjects.

Vocabulary: jobs and employment

4 Use words from this list to complete the sentences below. Use a dictionary to help you.

job career occupation temporary
permanent unemployed unskilled
manual work skilled professional full-time
self-employed part-time

a Jane has got a *temporary* job. She's working for two weeks while the receptionist is on holiday.
b Ralph has been ..... since he lost his job last year. He just can't find any work.
c He's got a ..... job. He only works ten hours a week.
d I have plenty of work and I can do most of it at home. I'm ....., so I'm my own boss.
e Margaret decided that she couldn't work ..... after she had children. She decided to work two days a week.
f I'm hoping to have a ..... in medicine. I want to become a surgeon.
g 'What do you do?' means 'What's your .....?' or 'What's your .....?'
h You've had six employers in the last two years. It's time you found a ..... job!

5 Put the jobs below into three categories:

carpenter lawyer labourer teacher
accountant plumber telephone engineer
cleaner doctor journalist

a unskilled manual worker
b skilled manual worker
c professional

6 Work in pairs. Find words from Exercises 4 and 5 to describe these jobs.

a 40 hours a week July–September cleaning in a factory
   full-time temporary cleaner
b 8 hours a week all year, teaching children
c 40 hours a week all year, putting in new telephone lines
d 40 hours a week, checking financial accounts (working for yourself)

Speaking: describing jobs

7 Describe the jobs of people you know to your partner. Don't say the name of the job. Can your partner guess the job?

EXAMPLE: *My friend works 35 hours a week in an office.*
Is she a full-time secretary?

Talking point

COMPANIES GIVE PART-TIME JOBS BECAUSE THEY DON'T WANT TO PAY YOU WHEN YOU GET SICK.

What do *you* think?

Action C

Applying for a job

- Listen to a job interview
- Write a CV
- Write an accompanying letter
- Vocabulary:
  useful expressions in
  business letters

Listening and Speaking: job interviews

1 🔊 **Listen to Gerald Sharp talking about his education and employment history. Look at his CV. What is the missing information?**

Curriculum Vitae

Personal information

Name: Gerald Sharp
Address: 128 Park Avenue, Swansea, SA2 9AR
Telephone: (01792) 266830
Age: 24   Date of birth: February 3rd 1973
Male/Female: Male

Educational qualifications
....

Career history
....

Skills
- Languages: German, Turkish
- I am familiar with a number of word-processing and accounting programs for PC and Macintosh.
- I have a full international driving licence.

Referees
Mrs A. Taylor, Sales Director, Short Breaks, 83 High Street, Swansea, SA1 6GH
Mr P. Elliott, General Manager, Three Towers Group, Tower House,
47 Castle Street, Cardiff CA1 8TF

A

(a) 14B Page Street
    Eaton
    Ipswich IP4 3SG
    England

(b) June 25th 1997

(c) The Personnel Manager
(d) IPF Leisure
    24 Boulevard St Michel
    Paris 75005
    France

    Dear Sir/Madam

(e) I am writing to apply for the post of Executive Secretary as advertised in the *London Evening News* on June 24th.

(f) I enclose my CV and look forward to hearing from you.

(g) Yours faithfully

(h) P.G. West (Ms)

2 **Make notes on your own education and career history. If it is not very interesting, improve it!**

3 **Work in pairs. Ask your partner questions about his / her education, work and skills. Then complete a CV for your partner.**

Reading accompanying letters

4 **Look at these two letters. What is their purpose?**

B

Morag Findlay
Music Stand
62 High Street
Witney OX8 6HJ

18 Aland Court
London SE16 1LA
March 1st 1997

Dear Ms Findlay,
    I am writing to apply for the post of shop assistant as advertised in your window this week.
    I enclose my curriculum vitae and look forward to hearing from you.

Yours sincerely,

Jania Fiddle (Ms)

5 Look at the letters again.

a When you write a business letter to someone, and you don't know the person's name, how do you start the letter:

• if it is to a man?
• if it is to a woman?
• if you don't know whether it is to a man or a woman?

b How do you end the letter if:
• you write to a person using their name?
• you don't use the person's name?

c Find this information in each letter.
• the date
• the writer's name
• the reason for writing
• the writer's address
• the job title of the person receiving the letter
• a reference to another document
• the address of the person receiving the letter

Writing an accompanying letter

6 Look at this job advertisement. Imagine you want to apply for the job. Write a letter to accompany your CV. Make sure you refer to any other things you need to enclose. Use expressions from the Phrasebook.

7 After writing your letter, exchange letters with your partner. Check:

• that the letter is organised in the same way as the letters opposite.
• that other documents are referred to.
• that expressions from the Phrasebook are used correctly.
• that the vocabulary and grammar are correct.

Phrasebook

Formal letters

Dear Sir / Madam
I am writing to apply for the post of secretary.
I enclose my curriculum vitae.
I look forward to hearing from you.
Yours faithfully
Yours sincerely

European Headquarters of a leading American Manufacturer of medical instruments based in Meudon (France) is looking for a

BILINGUAL EXECUTIVE SECRETARY

for the President Europe

English / French

Reporting to the President, you will be in constant relation with European subsidiaries and our US Headquaters. French mother tongue with an excellent level of English, you are 30 – 35 years old and have previous experience in a similar position. You have good skills in English shorthand and word processing (Word / Excel on Macintosh).
Well-organised, very flexible and perfect presentation. Please send your application form (letter, CV, photograph and current salary) under ref: 654 to INTERSEC, 36 rue de Paris, Meudon 92190 (France).

Word file   Unit 14

EDUCATION	WORK	
A level	accountant	unskilled (work)
BA	career	waitress
BSc	film editor	
certificate	journalist	**OTHER**
degree	manual (work)	admire
diploma	occupation	by chance
GCSE	permanent	client
grade	personal assistant	computer program
MA	(PA)	for
MBA	self-employed	since
MEd	skilled (work)	
MSc	temporary	
PGCE	tourist guide	
PhD	translator	
qualification	unemployed	

Grammar *backup 14*

Present perfect: *for* and *since*

Practice

1 *For* or *since*?

a since 1983
b ..... last Friday
c ..... the day before yesterday
d ..... three months
e ..... most of my life
f ..... the beginning of August
g ..... five minutes
h ..... the moment I saw her
i ..... a week
j ..... I started my new job

2 Write the <u>underlined</u> short forms in full.

a She <u>hasn't</u> come. has not
b <u>I've</u> met him before.
c <u>He's</u> left.
d They <u>haven't</u> arrived.
e <u>We've</u> known him for years.
f You <u>haven't</u> been there, have you?

3 Write sentences using the present perfect and *for* or *since*.

a I / be here / Wednesday
   I've been here since Wednesday.
b She / live / this house / ten years
c I / not see my sister / February
d He / have his job / the beginning of 1996
e We / not speak to him / last Tuesday

4 Translation

Write these sentences in your own language.

a I saw him yesterday.
b I haven't seen him since yesterday.
c I haven't seen him for a week.
d She's worked in an office since she was sixteen.
e She worked in an office when she was sixteen.
f She's worked in an office for sixteen years.

Reference

We use the present perfect with **for** and **since** to talk about situations that started in the past and are continuing now.

EXAMPLES: *I've been here **since** Tuesday.*
           (I am still here.)
           *He has lived here **for** about five years.*
           (He still works here.)

We use **for** when we refer to periods of time.

EXAMPLES: *She's worked there **for a month**.*
           *They've lived there **for many years**.*

We use **since** when we refer to points in time.

EXAMPLES: *I have loved her **since the day I met her**.*
           *He's been my friend **since 1990**.*

Short forms

The auxiliary **have** is often shortened in the present perfect in speech and informal writing.

EXAMPLES: ***You've** shown me.*
           (You have shown me.)
           *It **hasn't** left.*
           (It has not left.)

Irregular verbs

Practice

1 Which of these verbs have the same form for the past simple and past participle?

a teach   d stand
b pay   e drink
c know   f have

2 Find the past simple form of these verbs.

a drive   c shut
b take   d think

3 Find the past participle of these verbs.

a fall   c go
b write   d make

4 What are the infinitives of these verbs?

a worn   c brought
b begun   d rose

Reference

You need to learn the past simple form and the past participle of these verbs. They do not end in -ed and the past simple form is usually different from the past participle.

Infinitive	Past simple	Past participle	Infinitive	Past simple	Past participle
be	was/were	been	meet	met	met
become	became	become	pay	paid	paid
begin	began	begun	put	put	put
bring	brought	brought	read	read	read
build	built	built	rise	rose	risen
buy	bought	bought	say	said	said
come	came	come	see	saw	seen
do	did	done	sell	sold	sold
drink	drank	drunk	send	sent	sent
drive	drove	driven	shut	shut	shut
eat	ate	eaten	sleep	slept	slept
fall	fell	fallen	speak	spoke	spoken
find	found	found	spend	spent	spent
get	got	got	stand	stood	stood
give	gave	given	take	took	taken
go	went	gone	teach	taught	taught
have	had	had	tell	told	told
keep	kept	kept	think	thought	thought
know	knew	known	understand	understood	understood
leave	left	left	wear	wore	worn
make	made	made	write	wrote	written

15

An executive secretary

- Read a job history
- Take dictation
- Check and clarify information
- Vocabulary:
  punctuation
- Grammar:
  reported instructions and
  requests

Discussion: an executive secretary

1 What does an executive secretary do? What skills and personal qualities does an executive secretary need, do you think?

Listening to an interview

2 Listen to Eugénie Blanco talking about her job at the International Herald Tribune offices in Paris.

Part 1

Choose the correct answers.

a Eugénie works for the head of:
  - international sales.
  - national advertising.
  - international advertising.

b Eugénie talks about:
  - doing internal paperwork.
  - arranging her boss's agenda.
  - travelling with her boss.
  - booking his flights.
  - doing all his work when he's away.
  - booking his hotels.
  - taking his phone calls.

Part 2

Write the answers.

c Which three personal qualities does Eugénie think are important in an executive secretary?

d Where is Eugénie from? What languages does she speak?

e Where is her boss from?

Magazine 56

Eugénie Blanco

'I left Venezuela after High School and went to the States and did a two-year business course. Then I worked in an oil company for about four years. My first job was as a receptionist, but then they asked me to replace a senior secretary. Then I moved to London and worked for Marks & Spencer.

When I came to France, I got an ordinary secretarial job at the Venezuelan Embassy. But two weeks later they asked me to be secretary to the Ambassador! I did that for four years here in Paris. Then I decided I would like to work at the airport for Venezuelan Airlines. I started the job and soon after they told me to go and work as a senior secretary in the Head Office. After that I joined the Herald Tribune – it's been nine years now. They wanted someone with Spanish mother tongue, good English and a knowledge of French. I love the job.

I have never found it difficult to get a job. All the doors have opened for me because of my languages: my English, my Spanish and my French. The languages have helped me to get the jobs. When I was younger it was very rare for Latin American people to have good English. I got my first job in the oil company because of my English, and languages have helped me ever since.'

Reading a job history

3 **Read about Eugénie.**

a Complete this chart with information about some of Eugénie's jobs.

organisation	position(s)	no. of years
oil company	.....	.....
Venezuelan Embassy	.....	.....
Venezuelan Airlines	.....	.....
International Herald Tribune	.....	.....

b What skill has helped Eugénie most to find jobs?

Grammar: reported instructions and requests

4 **Look at these extracts from the interview with Eugénie.**

They asked me to be secretary to the Ambassador! They told me to go and work as a senior secretary in the Head Office.

a In which sentence is Eugénie reporting:
  • an instruction?
  • a request?
b Which verb often introduces reported requests?
c Which verb often introduces reported instructions?
d What structure follows these reporting verbs?

5 **Report these instructions and requests. Imagine who the speaker is.**

EXAMPLES: *'Please, sit down.'*
The interviewer told me to sit down.
'Could you phone Janet?'
She asked me to phone Janet.

a 'I want you to clean the meeting room first.'
b 'Could you open the door for me, please?'
c 'Turn the lights off.'
d 'Leave your car in the car park.'
e 'Would you answer my phone for the next hour, please?'
f 'Could you work late this evening?'

6 **Work in pairs. Think of something that someone has recently asked you to do. (It can be something interesting, or very difficult, or very frightening). Tell your partner.**

EXAMPLE: *My friend asked me to travel round the world with her.*

Then tell the other people about your partner's reported request.

EXAMPLE: *His friend asked him to travel round the world with her.*

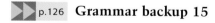 p.126 **Grammar backup 15**

Listening and Writing: dictation

7 🔊 **Look at the words below. Then listen and read. Find examples of each type of punctuation in the letter. Use a dictionary to help you.**

a question mark
b full stop
c capital letter
d comma
e quotation marks (inverted commas)
f exclamation mark

g semi-colon
h colon
i brackets
j apostrophe
k dash
l new paragraph
m heading

```
Dear Brian,

TRAVEL
I'm arriving on Sunday. My flight details are:
BA 457, arriving Dublin 09.30 (if it's not
late!). Can you meet me with a hire car -
nothing too expensive?

HOTEL
I'd like to stay at 'Polansky's' again; it was
fine last time. But please make sure it's a
quiet room.

I look forward to seeing you again and hearing
about developments in the Irish market.
```

8 **Listen to your teacher and write what he / she says. Use expressions from the Phrasebook to interrupt if you need to.**

Phrasebook

Taking dictation

Could you repeat the last sentence?
Could you speak a little more slowly?
Can you spell that please?
Has that got capital letters?
Is this a new paragraph?

Talking point

PEOPLE GIVE DICTATION BECAUSE IT MAKES THEM FEEL IMPORTANT. IT'S NOT NECESSARY THESE DAYS.

What do *you* think?

Action **B** # Culture matters

- Describe cultures, seasons and lifestyles
- Vocabulary:
  - adjectives for food
  - personal qualities
  - weather
  - geographical features

Discussion: generalising about foreign countries

1 We all make generalisations about other countries and the people who live in them. Often they are completely wrong! How do foreigners see you and your country? Choose two words to describe foreigners' ideas about these things in your country:

- the food.   • the weather.   • the people.   • geography.
- people's lifestyles.

Vocabulary: describing food

2 **Look at these words for describing food. Use a dictionary to help you.**

spicy   bland   delicious   tasty   dull   hot   varied

Find:
a two words that mean food tastes good.
b two words that mean food has very little taste.
c a word that can mean the same as *spicy*.
d a word that means there are a lot of different kinds of food.

3 **Describe what you know about food from some of these places.**

France   United States   Russia   China   Japan
Argentina   Mexico   Britain   Italy

Where do you think the food in the photographs is from?

Vocabulary: personal qualities

4 **Look at these words for describing personal qualities.**

cold   formal   quiet   kind   warm   informal   emotional
helpful   open   punctual   generous   (un)friendly
well-organised   mean   loud   polite

Use words from the box to complete these sentences. There is sometimes more than one correct answer.

a He's very *emotional*. He cries at weddings and even at the cinema!
b She's always on time. She's very ..... .
c Good personal assistants are ..... to their bosses.
d People who have very little money are often very ..... . They know how it feels to need something.
e He's very ..... . He never uses people's first names.
f Every piece of paper is filed in the right place. I'm very ..... .

Make sentences using the other words.

5 **Look at the pictures on the left. Say what you think.**

a Which countries are these people from? Why do you think that?
b Match the adjectives above with the people. Do you find this easy? Do you know people from these countries? Explain your choices to your partner.

Vocabulary: weather

6 Look at these words for describing the weather. Match each word with a picture.

hot   cold   mild   dry   wet   rainy
warm   windy   sunny   cloudy   fine

Speaking: describing seasons

7 Work in pairs.

a Look at the times of the seasons in Europe. Are they the same in your country?
   • SPRING: March – May
   • SUMMER: June – September
   • AUTUMN (*USA=Fall*) October – November
   • WINTER: December – February

b Describe the seasons in your country. What is the usual type of weather in each season? How does the weather change people's leisure activities?

Vocabulary: geographical features

8 Use these words to complete the sentences.

river   valley   mountain   plain   desert   coast

a The highest ..... in the world is in the Himalayas and is called Mount Everest.
b The longest ..... in the world is the Nile.
c You can find a ..... between two hills.
d Some countries do not have a ..... . Examples are Bolivia, Austria and Nepal.
e Saudi Arabia has a large ..... called The Empty Quarter.
f A ..... is a large area of flat land.

Reading and Speaking: lifestyles

9 Read these newspaper headlines.

A

SIX MORE DEAD IN CITY SHOOTINGS

B

THOUSANDS LIVING ON THE STREETS IN 97

C

Jobs That Can Kill You!

Now look at these words. Guess which words come from each article. (Some words can come from more than one article.)

rich   safe   poor   relaxed   wealthy
stressful   dangerous   homeless   unemployed
violent

Speaking: describing another country

10 Work in pairs. Choose a country that you both know something about. Choose words from Exercises 2 – 9 to describe the country and its people. Tell other people the words you have chosen. Can they guess the name of the country?

Being polite

- Use polite language
- Write a thank you letter
- Vocabulary:
  - polite phrases
- Grammar:
  - *to, because* and *for*

Discussion: politeness

1 **Politeness is a very important area of cultural difference. Read these comments about politeness in Britain.**

a What can you learn about British ideas of politeness? Does anything surprise you?

A

Italian journalist:
Beppe Severgnini, in his book *Inglesi*, writes: *Some time ago an Italian friend of mine made the following discovery: in Britain you need four 'thank yous' to buy a bus ticket. The bus conductor comes up and says the first 'thank you' (meaning 'I am here.'). The passenger hands over the money with another 'thank you' ('I can see you, here is the money.'). Another 'thank you' from the conductor ('Here is your ticket'). The passenger takes the ticket saying the final 'thank you'. You can total six 'thank yous' if you do not hand over the correct money and need change from the conductor.*

B

French businesswoman:
What I find strange about British people is that they always say 'I'm sorry'. French people don't keep saying sorry. We don't apologise all the time. Why do the British feel so guilty?

C

British shopkeeper:
A lot of people from outside Britain ... often they don't say 'please' or 'thank you' at all. I think it's terribly rude.

b Look at the situation in A. Compare this with the process of buying a bus (or train) ticket in your country. What are the differences?
c How and when do you apologise in your country?

Speaking: saying 'sorry'

2 **When people say 'sorry' in English, they are not always apologising. Match these situations with the pictures on the left.**

a apologising for your own mistake
b apologising before correcting another person's mistake
c interrupting someone
d asking for repetition
e asking for an explanation
f apologising for an accident
g disagreeing with someone

Do you use the same word for all these situations in your language?

SORRY, CAN I SAY SOMETHING?

1

SORRY!

2

SORRY, YOU'VE GIVEN ME THE WRONG CHANGE

3

SORRY, I SAID S6S2, BUT IT'S S662

4

SORRY, I DIDN'T HEAR THE QUESTION

5

SORRY, I DON'T UNDERSTAND

6

SORRY, I DON'T REALLY AGREE

7

Reading thank you letters

3 It is sometimes polite to write short 'thank you' letters. When do people write letters of thanks to friends or colleagues at work? Think of some situations.

4 Look at this letter. Who is the writer thanking and for what?

TELELAB

4, Crown Place
Norwich
NR2 3AX

August 24th 1997

Mr F. Keller
The Manager
Grand Hotel
Spiegelstrasse
Zurich

Dear Mr Keller
I am writing on behalf of Ms Jordan to thank you for returning her briefcase.
She is particularly grateful because the case contained a number of important documents. Ms Jordan is extremely relieved to have them back. Once again, thank you for your help and efficiency.

Yours sincerely

K Jones

K. Jones

Tel: 01603 99832

Fax: 01603 998313

5 Put these steps in the same order as in the letter.
The writer:
• explains why Ms Jordan is grateful.
• says thank you again.
• explains the reason for writing.

Grammar: *to, because* and *for*

6 Find phrases from the letter to answer these questions.
a (para. 1) Why is Mr Jones writing this letter?
b (para. 1) What does Ms Jordan thank Mr Keller for?
c (para. 2) Why is Ms Jordan particularly grateful?
d (para. 3) What else does Mr Jones thank Mr Keller for?

To, because and *for* are used here to give reasons.
What structures follow them?

7 Complete these sentences with *to, because* and *for.*
a Thank you very much ..... your gift.
b I am writing ..... there is a problem with our telephone line.
c We are writing ..... thank you all.
d Thank you ..... coming to an interview last week.
e She would like to thank you ..... helping her.
f Please thank your colleagues ..... all their hard work.
g He's here ..... I invited him.

▶▶ p.127 Grammar backup 15

Writing a thank you letter

8 Choose one of the following situations (or a real-life situation) and write a letter of thanks.

a You work for a charity. It pays for university courses for people from poor countries. A woman has just sent a large cheque to the charity. Write back on behalf of your boss.

b You work for Telelab. A man has written to the company to say that he thinks one of your products is wonderful. Your boss asks you to reply for her.

Word file Unit 15

OFFICE	WEATHER	OTHER
executive	cloudy	dangerous
secretary	dry	efficiency
internal	fine	extremely
paperwork	mild	guilty
senior	rainy	homeless
	sunny	on behalf of
FOOD	wet	particularly
bland	windy	relieved
delicious		safe
spicy	**SEASONS**	violent
tasty	autumn	wealthy
varied	spring	
	summer	
PERSONAL	winter	
QUALITIES		
emotional	**GEOGRAPHY**	
(in)formal	coast	
generous	desert	
loud	mountain	
mean	plain	
polite	river	
punctual	valley	
quiet		

Grammar *backup 15*

Reported instructions and requests

Practice

1 Complete the sentences with an object pronoun (*me / you / him / her / us / them*).

a I told them to stay.
   (George and Peter)
b She asked ..... to leave.
   (my sister and me)
c We asked ..... not to apply for the job.
   (Sally)
d They told ..... to open his bag. (Jeff)

2 Correct the mistakes in these reported instructions and requests.

a The receptionist asked her to sitting down.
   The receptionist asked her to sit down.
b I've told him wait.
c He's asking us to not smoke.
d The security guard told us not to using the lift.

3 Report these instructions and requests.

a Could you wait in reception? (female secretary to visitor)
   She asked him to wait in reception.
b Could you open the window, please? (woman to you)
c Please don't smoke during take-off. (air hostess to people on plane)
d Don't give that man a job! (man to woman)
e Office telephones are NOT for personal use. (male manager to staff)

4 Translation

   Write these sentences in your own language.

a We asked them not to arrive late.
b She told the dog to sit.
c I asked him not to wear those clothes.
d I told her to take notes.

Reference

We often use **tell** and **ask** to report instructions and requests.

EXAMPLES: *He **told** me to work late.*
           *I **asked** her to start early.*

Instructions

Tell is always followed by an object.

EXAMPLE: *She told **you** to write the report.*

The object is often followed by **to + infinitive**.

EXAMPLE: *She told us **to help** you.*

We report a negative instruction by adding **not** before **to + infinitive**.

EXAMPLE: *He told me **not to wait**.*

Requests

Structures with **ask** follow the same pattern as structures with **tell**.

EXAMPLES: *She asked **them to wait.***
           *He asked **Sally not to go.***

In a work situation there is sometimes very little difference between a polite instruction and a request. So when we report them, we can use **tell** or **ask** for both instructions and requests.

to, because and for

Practice

1 Complete these with *to* or *because*.

a I left early to go to another meeting.

b The receptionist has gone out ..... she had to go to the dentist.

c I am writing ..... thank you for the gift.

d I am waiting ..... I want to lock the office.

2 Complete these sentences with a reason.

a People take holidays to ...

b I'm studying English because ...

c I want to go to the United States to ...

d I'd like to have a good salary because ...

3 Write two sentences in response to each situation. Use:

- *for* + noun phrase
- *for* + -ing

a Someone sent you a book.
Thank you for the book.
Thank you for sending the book.

b Someone bought you a ticket for a concert.

c Someone helped you when you were on a trip.

d Someone gave you flowers.

e Someone invited you to lunch.

4 Translation

Write these sentences in your own language.

a I'm writing to ask about your plans.

b I'm writing because I have heard about your new job.

c Thank you for offering me the job.

d Thank you for your advice.

Reference

To, **because** and **for** are all used to give reasons.

To is followed by an infinitive when it is used to give a reason.

EXAMPLES: *I am writing **to complain**.*
*I went to Munich **to meet** a customer.*

Because is usually followed by a clause.

EXAMPLES: *I was late **because the train didn't come**.*
*She's here **because she wants to see the manager**.*

When we say **thank you** we often use **for** to introduce the reason for our thanks. **Thank you for ...** is followed by a noun phrase or by a verb with an **-ing** ending.

EXAMPLES: *Thank you for **your help**.*
*Thank you for **your card**.*
*Thank you for **sending** the report.*
*Thank you for **replying** quickly.*

THANK YOU FOR COMING!

AND THANK YOU SO MUCH FOR THE GIFT.

Procedures

16

Action **A** # Selling advertising

- Understand job descriptions
- Report messages and conversations
- Grammar:
  reporting speech with
  present tense verbs

Reading and Listening: an interview

1 **Véronique Feldmann works for the International Herald Tribune. Read about her job and choose answers to these questions.**

a Does Véronique work in:
   - the Marketing Department?
   - the Sports Department?
   - the Supplements Department?

b Which of the pictures above shows an example of Véronique's work?

c Does an Advertising Coordinator:
   - write articles?
   - sell advertising?
   - organise advertising?

d Is an IHT supplement:
   - a part of the main newspaper?
   - an extra part of the newspaper?
   - the normal advertising section?

e Are the supplements paid for by:
   - the newspaper?
   - advertisers?
   - journalists?

'I work in the Supplements Department. I'm the Advertising Coordinator, and my job is to produce the advertising supplements. A supplement is like a newspaper inside the main newspaper and we call it a 'sponsored section' because it is financed by the advertisers. We only have these supplements if we can sell enough advertising.

For a sponsored section we think of an idea, then we sell the advertising space and get articles, photographs, illustrations. Then we do the layout. We put the whole supplement together in this department. The supplements don't appear every day – we usually do about 200 a year.'

2 **Work in pairs. Discuss possible answers to these questions about Véronique's job.**

a Do you think the newspaper sells advertising outside France?

b The IHT produces *subject supplements* and *country supplements*. What do you think the differences are?

c What languages does she need for her job?

d Does Véronique sell space *directly* to companies?

e Why does she need to speak to reps before she decides on a subject for an international supplement?

3 🔊 **Listen to Véronique.**

a Part 1. Were your answers to a and b above correct?

b Part 2. Were your answers to c – e above correct?

c What subjects do you think make good advertising supplements?

Grammar: reporting speech with present tense verbs

4 **Look at these sentences. Véronique is reporting routine conversations with her colleagues.**

A *'Sometimes they say that it's a problem.'*
B *'They tell me that they can sell half a page.'*
C *'I ask him how many pages he can sell.'*
D *'They want to know if they can have more time.'*

a Which word follows *tell* in reported statements? Does this type of word also follow *say*?

b Rewrite sentence A using *tell* instead of *say*. Rewrite B using *say* instead of *tell*.

c Compare the structure of the questions below with the reported questions in C and D.
'How many pages can you sell?'
'Can we have more time?'

5 **Write these words in the correct order to make reported questions.**

a He wants to know / you can finish / if / the report / today /.
He wants to know if you can finish the report today.

b He wants to know / his desk / where / has gone /.

c She is asking / you can meet her / when /.

d They want to know / a photocopier / we have got / if /.

6 **Véronique's assistant is speaking to a rep on the phone. The assistant reports the conversation to Véronique and then reports back to the rep. Write the assistant's words.**

Rep: I can sell about half a page on banking.
Assistant to Véronique: He says he can sell about half a page on banking.
Véronique: Ask him if he can sell it before next week.
Assistant to rep: Can ..... ?
Rep: I think I need more time.
Assistant to Véronique: ..... .
Véronique: How much more time?
Assistant to rep: Véronique ..... .
Rep: I can do it in two weeks.
Assistant to Véronique: ..... .
Véronique: That's fine.
Assistant to rep: ..... .

🔊 **Listen and check. Then act out the conversations in groups of three.**

▶▶ p.134 **Grammar backup 16**

Speaking: reporting messages

7 **Work in pairs.**
A: Turn to page 139.
B: You are the director's assistant, and your boss is abroad. When he / she telephones, use your notes below to report the messages. Then change roles, and telephone your partner to get your messages.

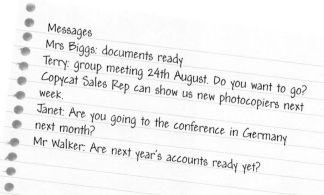

Messages
Mrs Biggs: documents ready
Terry: group meeting 24th August. Do you want to go?
Copycat Sales Rep can show us new photocopiers next week.
Janet: Are you going to the conference in Germany next month?
Mr Walker: Are next year's accounts ready yet?

Action **B** # Putting it together

- Describe position and layout
- Vocabulary:
  - features of a newspaper page
  - businesses and business areas

Vocabulary: features of a newspaper page

1 Look at the page from a sponsored section on Asian / American business that appeared in the *International Herald Tribune*. Find these newspaper features. Use a dictionary to help you.

an advertisement   an illustration   a pie chart   a headline
an article   a photograph

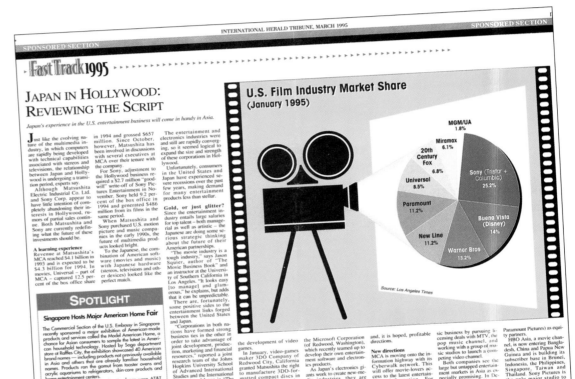

Speaking: describing position and layout

2 Use these expressions to complete the sentences below. How much space does each feature take in the sponsored section on the opposite page?

> a whole page   (about) half a page
> a quarter of a page

a   The NEC advertisement takes a quarter of a page.
b   The illustration and chart take ..... .
c   The article 'Japan in Hollywood' (with the illustration and chart) takes ..... .
d   The sponsored section takes ..... .

3 Describe where each feature is on the page. Use these words and phrases.

above

at the top (of the page)
in the middle / centre   next to
on the left   on the right
at the bottom

below

a   The chart is at the top of the page, on the right.
b   The advertisement for NEC ..... .
c   The 'Spotlight' article ..... .
d   The 'Japan in Hollywood' headline ..... .
e   The illustration ..... .
f   The photograph of a man on his hotel balcony ..... .

Talking point

NOBODY SHOULD WORK LATE IF THEY AREN'T PAID FOR IT.

What do *you* think?

Vocabulary: business areas

4 When Véronique has an idea for a new sponsored section, she sends a proposal to the reps. The proposal lists subjects for the section.

a   Look at the front page of her proposal. Is this a subject supplement or a country supplement?

Herald INTERNATIONAL Tribune

The International Herald Tribune proposes to publish a sponsored section on

M A L A Y S I A

b   Read these headings from her proposal. Group the businesses below under one or more headings. Use a dictionary to help you.

A Telecommunications   E   Banking and
B Services   Finance
C Exporting   F   Tourism
D Energy

> insurance companies   hotels
> translation agencies   mobile phone suppliers
> clothes manufacturers   travel agencies
> investment companies   satellite TV stations
> telephone companies   transportation companies
> oil companies   toy manufacturers   airlines
> office furniture suppliers   software companies

Discussion: planning a sponsored section

5 Write a list of headings for your own country (perhaps including headings A – F above). Then think of particular businesses to feature under each of your headings.

Finishing touches

Listening: creating a supplement

1 **Put these different stages of Véronique's work in the correct order.**

a The reps visit companies to discuss the supplement.
b Véronique has an idea for a supplement.
c The reps identify possible advertisers.
d The reps agree that the idea is a good one.

What do you think the next stage is?

2 🔊 **Listen and check the next stage in the process. Were you correct?**

3 🔊 **Look at the pictures and listen again.**

A

B

C

a What does Véronique say is the correct order for these three stages?
b What two short forms does Véronique use for the word *advertisement*?
c Why do you think she says the advertising layout is like a puzzle?

Reading and Speaking: making suggestions

4 **Two people are working on another newspaper. They are trying to decide where to put advertisements on a page. Read part of their conversation and find three suggestions.**

Paul:	Let's put it there, at the bottom, on the left.
Angela:	Here? OK. That looks fine.
Paul:	And shall we put this one at the top?
Angela:	Hmm. No, I don't think so. Why don't we put it at the bottom next to the other one.
Paul:	Where? On the right?
Angela:	Yes. What do you think?
Paul:	OK. Yes, they look good next to each other ...

5 **Work in pairs. Look at the layout of the page below. Read the editor's comments about the design of the page.**

a How can you change the layout to satisfy the editor? Make suggestions by using expressions from the Phrasebook.

b Draw your new layout on a piece of paper.

'NO, NO, NO. IT LOOKS TERRIBLE. PUT THE ARTICLE NEARER TO THE MIDDLE OF THE PAGE ... AND CHANGE THE POSITION OF THE PHOTOGRAPH. AND THOSE TWO CAR HIRE ADS ARE TOO CLOSE TOGETHER. PUT ONE AT THE TOP OF THE PAGE AND ONE NEAR THE BOTTOM.'

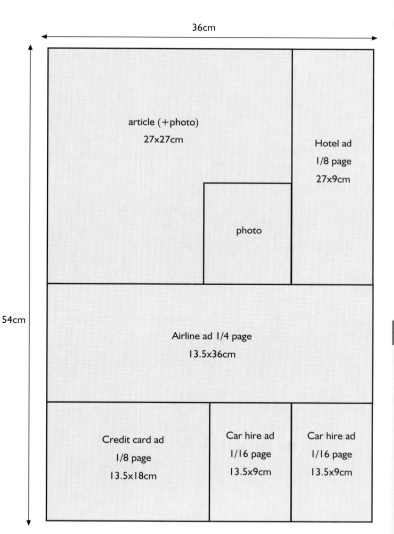

Phrasebook

Making suggestions

Shall we start now?
Yes, let's.
Let's use the meeting room.
OK.
Why don't we ask Paula to come?
That's a good idea.

Speaking: describing a layout

6 **Describe your new layout to the class. Has any pair drawn a different layout from yours?**

Reading: checking text

7 **Sometimes mistakes appear in newspapers. There are five in this advertisement. Find them and correct them.**

SECRETARIAL SERVICES

Experienced secretary will type allyour document accurately and fast on a word word processor. Freindly, reliable, profesional service.
Tel/fax 634192 after 6 p.m.

Word file Unit 16

NEWSPAPERS	below	satellite TV
ad	in the centre	station
advert	in the middle	software
advertisement	next to	supplier
advertising	on the left	telecommu-
article	on the right	nications
headline	to the left (of)	tourism
illustration	to the right (of)	toy
layout	whole page	transportation
photograph		
sponsored section	**BUSINESSES**	**JOBS**
supplement	**AND**	coordinator
	BUSINESS	rep (representative)
PAGE LAYOUT	**ACTIVITIES**	
above	agency	
at the bottom	airline	
at the top	exporting	

Grammar *backup 16*

Reporting speech with present tense verbs

Practice

1 Complete these sentences with *asks*, *says* or *tells*.

a He ..... he'll be late.
b Véronique ..... the reps when she needs the adverts.
c She ..... the reps if the subject is going to be difficult to sell.

2 Add the right word to these reported questions.

a 'When are you coming?' He wants to know *when* you are coming.
b 'Has the meeting finished?' He wants to know ..... the meeting has finished.
c 'What's the problem?' He is asking ..... the problem is.
d 'Why are we doing a supplement on holidays now?' She wants to know ..... we're doing a supplement on holidays now.

3 Report these sentences.

a 'It's raining.' He .....
   He says that it's raining.
b 'My flight arrives at 8.00 p.m.' She .....
c 'Where is the Regent Hotel?' They .....
d 'Can she meet me this evening?' He .....
e 'How many adverts do you need?' They .....

4 Translation

Write these sentences in your own language.

a He says that you enjoy your job.
b People ask why I work here.
c We want to know if you're happy in this department.
d She tells me that you're enjoying the work.

Reference

We use present tense reporting verbs to report recent or routine statements or questions. We often use:

• **say** or **tell** to report statements.
• **want to know** or **ask** to report questions.

Reporting statements

Note the structures that follow **say** and **tell**:

EXAMPLES: He **says (that)** he's coming now.
They often **tell us (that)** the job is urgent.

The object that follows **tell** is a pronoun (e.g. me), a noun (e.g. the staff) or a name (e.g. Tania).

Reporting questions

Note the structures that follow **want to know** and **ask**:

She	wants to know is asking (them)	if when why	the doors are open.

We report questions that begin with **when**, **what**, **why** etc using:

• the same **wh-** question word.
• the word order of a statement (not the word order of a question).

EXAMPLE: **'When is** the meeting?'
She wants to know **when** the meeting **is**.

If there is no **wh-** question word at the start of the question, we usually report it using:

• **if** + the word order of a statement (not the word order of a question).

EXAMPLES: **'Can he** come?'
They are asking **if he can** come.
'Do you want some coffee?'
He wants to know **if you want** some coffee.

David Ellis works for DEECO Ltd as an administrative assistant. One of his jobs is to open the mail in the morning.

1 **Look at some of today's mail on this page and the next. Which:**

a asks for payment?

b does David not open? Why?

c go to Suzanne Davies?

d go to Bill Giles?

e is probably thrown away?

f does David deal with himself?

2 **Look at message C. Work in pairs.**

A: You are David. Call Sarah Peters' secretary and arrange a meeting as soon as possible.

B: You are Sarah Peters' secretary. Talk to David and agree a time and place for the meeting.

3 **Look at message E. You are David. Write a note to Ms Davies giving her this information.**

4 **Look at fax F and note J. Do what Ms Davies asks. Write an accompanying letter to go with the report.**

5 **Look at fax A. The hotel has made a mistake with Mr Giles' reservation. Write a fax to the hotel to explain that Mr Giles wants to stay for three nights, not two. The arrival date is correct, but he wants to stay until the 27th. Then write a note to Bill Giles. Tell him what you have done and attach fax A.**

6 **Look at invoice G. You now have a cheque from the Finance Department. Write a letter to World Travel enclosing the cheque. Make up an address for World Travel.**

A

FAX

TO: B. Giles
FROM: The Grand Hotel
NO. OF PAGES: 1

FAX NO.: 0171 222 5904
DATE: July 2nd

SUBJECT: **Confirmation of reservation / Mr Giles**

This is to confirm the reservation for Mr B. Giles for two nights, arriving July 24 and departing July 26, for one double room at £110 a night plus taxes.

B Personal

Ms S. Davies
DEECO Ltd
Churchill House
Rupert Square
London NW1 4GQ

MESSAGE

C

To: David
From: Suzanne

Date: 1/7
Time: 6.00 p.m.

Could you call Sarah Peters' secretary at Mainline and arrange an urgent meeting with her? I'm free for the next two days.

MEMORANDUM

July 1st

Suzanne

Frank Carter at City Bank is very interested in some of our new products and would like to call in and speak to you some time next week. Could you call him and arrange it?

John

D

E

MESSAGE

To: David
From: Bill Giles

Date: 2/7
Time: 8.15 a.m.

Sheila called this morning to say she is sick and can't come to work today. Can you let Ms Davies know, please?

H

Reply in seven days and receive a free gift

Suzanne Davies
Marketing Department
DEECO Ltd
Churchill House
Rupert Square
London NW1 4GQ

F

FAX

TO: Suzanne Davies, Marketing
FROM: Pat Turner, Finance
DATE: 2/7
PAGES: 1

I haven't received your budget figures for next year yet. I need them <u>urgently</u> and no later than tomorrow, please.

I

Dear Mr Giles

I enclose the minutes of last week's meeting of Business Forum. The next meeting will be held on September 7th at the Clarendon Hotel.

Yours sincerely

F Scott-Mackenzie

F Scott-Mackenzie

INVOICE

No. 6358
To: Mr B. Giles, DEECO Ltd
From: World Travel
Date: 1/7/97

For:
Plane tickets for Mr Giles
London – Miami – Buenos Aires –
Santiago – New York – London

Total: £3156.00

G

David

Please post the figures to Pat Turner in the Finance Department as soon as possible.
Suzanne

J

Suzanne Davies
Marketing Department
DEECO Ltd
Churchill House
Rupert Square
London NW1 4GQ

K

Information for pairwork

Unit 1B page 9
Speaking: sharing information

4 A: Ask your partner for the information that he / she has. Then answer his / her questions, using the information below.

Model:	Rover Metro
Age:	4 years
Price:	£4,500
Telephone number:	01865 334421

When you finish, check your answers with your partner.

Unit 1C page 11
Speaking: giving and taking an order

7 A: You are a shop assistant. The instrument the customer asks for is not in stock. Ask questions and complete an order form. Start like this:
Good morning. Can I help you?

Customer Order
Name: ....
Address: ....
....
Tel: ....
Item: ....
Price: ....

Unit 2A page 15
Listening and Speaking: telling the time

7 A: Answer your partner's questions with this information:

- party: 8.00 p.m.
- film: 6.15 p.m.

EXAMPLE: *What time is the train?*
At quarter past three.

Then ask your partner about the times of:

- the bus
- the meeting

Write the answers.

Unit 2C page 19
Speaking: describing jobs

8 A: Answer your partner's questions. Use the information below. Then ask questions about your partner's job and complete the notes below. Use expressions from the Phrasebook.

	A	B
job?	supermarket manager	
place?	supermarket	
full-time?	yes	
start?	8.00 a.m.	
finish?	6.00 p.m.	
weekends?	yes (Saturday)	
like job?	yes	

Unit 3A page 23
Speaking: asking questions

11 A: You are a shop assistant in a music shop. Answer your customer's questions about the things you have got in the shop.

EXAMPLE: *Have you got any guitar strings?*
Yes, we have. / I'm sorry. We haven't.

in stock
- violin cases
- CDs
- cassette recorders

not in stock
- guitar strings
- songbooks

Unit 3C *page 27*
Speaking about present activities

7 A: There are six differences between the picture on this page and your partner's picture. Ask and answer questions about the people in the picture to find the differences.

EXAMPLE: *Is Alan talking to Teresa?*
No, he isn't. He's ...

Unit 4C *page 35*
Speaking: a job interview

8 A: You are interviewing your partner for the job in advertisement A. Ask about personal details, skills and interests. Is he / she a good person for the job? Answer his / her questions with this information about the job:

Salary: £10,000 a year
Holidays: 4 weeks
Hours: 8.00 p.m. – 2.00 a.m.

A
**Bar staff wanted for busy
night club in luxury hotel
Apply to: Box 133**

Now change roles. Apply for the job in advertisement B. At the end of the interview, ask about the salary, holidays and working hours.

B
**Small, friendly travel agency needs new
staff. No experience necessary.
Apply to: Box 782**

Unit 5C *page 43*
Speaking: welcoming a visitor at reception

6 A: Look at the page from your diary and your business card below. You have an appointment at the Bank of Europe. Talk to the receptionist. Then change roles.

Unit 6B *page 49*
Speaking: answering the telephone

7 A: You have a number of sports shops. Telephone the sports equipment manufacturer, Sport Ace, and ask for the General Manager.

Unit 6C *page 51*
Speaking: making appointments

6 A: Mr Ellison is your boss and you have his diary. Write some appointments in Mr Ellison's diary. Leave some spaces. Answer your partner's telephone call.

Unit 7A *page 55*
Speaking: arranging a meeting

8 **A:** You are Mr Shaw's secretary. Ms Pawlowska's secretary telephones you to arrange a meeting. You know the secretary well. Look at Mr Shaw's diary below and arrange a meeting.

APRIL

Monday 11

Out all day – seminar at Chamber of Commerce

Tuesday 12

8.00 – 11.00 a.m. interviews
2.00 – 6.00 p.m. interviews

Wednesday 13

11.00 a.m. – 1.00 p.m. Sales Conference
4.00 – 6.00 p.m. interviews

Unit 7C *page 59*
Speaking: booking a hotel room

6 **A:** Telephone the Royal Hotel to make a booking. Answer the receptionist's questions.

Project 1 *page 103*

3 **A:** You are David Long's secretary. Lorna Davies' secretary telephones about a meeting. Look at David Long's diary and confirm the time of the meeting.

Monday	**11 June**
2.00 – 5.30 Team meeting. Rm 1Y	

Tuesday	**12 June**
9. 00 – 12.00 Pete Fallows	
2.00 – 5.00 p.m. Progress meeting Rm 1Y	

Wednesday	**13 June**
Paris	

Thursday	**14 June**
3.00 – 5.00 p.m. Presentation skills course	

Friday	**15 June**
3.00 – 5.00 p.m. Presentation skills course	

Unit 16 *page 129*
Speaking: reporting messages

8 **A:** You are the director of a company and you are on a business trip. Phone your assistant and ask if there are any messages for you. Take notes. Invent answers to any questions.

Then change roles. You are an assistant and your boss telephones you. Give him / her the messages below.

MESSAGES

MR ROGERS: WHEN DO YOU WANT TO
START YOUR COMPUTER COURSE?
JANE LLOYD: THE STATISTICS FOR YOUR
REPORT ARE READY.
PETER MITCHELL: HE CAN MEET YOU
NEXT MONDAY OR TUESDAY
MRS RICHARDS: HAVE YOU FINISHED
YOUR MARKETING PLAN YET?
LISA: SHE WANTS TO TAKE TWO WEEKS
HOLIDAY IN JULY. OK?

Tapescripts

Unit 1A Exercise 5 *page 7*
(C = customer, M = Morag)
C: Good morning.
M: Good morning. Can I help you?
C: Yes, please. Er, have you got a white Fender guitar?
M: Yes, we have. It's in the back. Just a minute … Here it is.
C: How much is it?
M: £350. The same as the black one.
C: Right. I'll take it.
M: Oh good. It's a beautiful guitar. How are you paying?
C: By credit card. Is that OK?
M: Yes, sure.
C: Here you are.
M: Thanks. Sign there, please. Right. Your receipt. And your guitar.
C: Thank you. Goodbye.
M: Goodbye.

Unit 1B Exercise 1 *page 8*
a The first ball is number … 30. Here comes the second ball … number 41. Now, the next one … number 11. The fourth number is … number 46. Now we have number … 16. And finally … number 22.
b The first ball is number … 37. Here comes the second ball … number 12. Now, the next one … number 28. The fourth number is … number 46. Now we have number … 49. And finally … number 3.

Unit 1B Exercise 3 *page 8*
1 It's an ADN 486.
2 This one's £33.50.
3 It's 0171 for London, then 639 4588.
4 We're at number 27.
5 FA 338 for Paris.
6 Yes, December 1973.
7 It's only £129.99.
8 And number 000594.
9 That's right. 1968.
10 Yes, it's 4129 8735 0061 9432.

Unit 1B Exercise 5 *page 9*
1 What, the microphone? It's sixty-three pounds ninety-eight.
2 I'll check … Yes, the drum kit costs seven hundred and sixty-eight pounds.
3 This music stand? Let's have a look. Yes, it costs thirty-two twenty-five.
4 Three thousand seven hundred pounds for that piano, but that's a good price.
5 Yes, each piece of music is two ninety-nine. Is that all right?

Unit 1B Exercise 7 *page 9*
(C = customer, M = Morag)
C: Have you got an X50 keyboard.
M: No, but I can order it for you.
C: Fine. Thanks.
M: Right … can I take some details then. What's your name?
C: Batey … Alison Batey. That's B-A-T-E-Y.
M: Alison Batey. OK. And your address?
C: 296 Corn Street.
M: In Witney …
C: Yes.

M: Have you got a telephone number?
C: Yes. My number's 916733.
M: 916733. Good. Right I'll just check the catalogue. So … you want the X50 keyboard. Let me see. Here it is … £449.00. (X50 … £449.00.) Now, how much deposit would you like to pay?
C: Er … a hundred pounds?
M: Yes, that's fine.

Unit 1C Exercise 2 *page 10*
a A: How do you spell Thompson?
   B: That's T-H-O-M-P-(pause)-S-O-N.
b No, Hyde. H-Y-D-E.
c Sheep. S-H-double E-P.
d A: Can you spell Tennison for me?
   B: Yes, it's with an I: T-E-double N-I-S-O-N.
e No, not Harper – Carter. C-A-R-T-E-R.
f My name's Maggie Frazer – that's spelt F-R-A-Z-E-R.

Unit 1C Exercise 3 *page 10*
1 No, I don't live in Witney – I'm from Oxford. The address is 15 Magdalen Road – that's M-A-G-D-A-L-E-N, Magdalen Road. And I'm Simon Green.
2 It's Rowley, Susan Rowley. Rowley's spelt R-O-W-L-E-Y. I'm from here in Witney – 14B, Thame Street, Yes. T-H-A-M-E – that's right.

Unit 2A Exercise 6 *page 15*
a A: Come at quarter to eight on Monday morning.
   B: Quarter to eight! That's rather early!
b He can't come in the morning, but he's free at half past two.
c I'm in the office between 2.00 and 5.30 on Tuesday afternoon.
d I'll see you at the theatre at twenty past seven. Don't be late!
e The meeting usually finishes between 4.30 and 5.00.

Unit 2B Exercise 10 *page 17*
Unlock the till with your key, but remember: don't leave your key in the till. Press the buttons for each item, like this. Then, press the TOTAL button – here – and the drawer opens. Put the money in: twenties here, tens there. And take out the change. Give the receipt to the customer with the change. Don't leave the till open. Always close it. OK? Now you try.

Unit 3B Exercise 1 *page 24*
(C = caller, J = John)
C: So what's your new recording studio like?
J: Well, it's very colourful! The walls are black and I've got a red carpet on the floor. The door's a sort of purple colour …
C: Purple?
J: Yes, why not? And I've got a yellow sofa …
C: A yellow sofa?
J: Yes, and that's not all. The pink shelves look nice by the window. Oh and there's a blue desk … but everything else is quite ordinary.

C: What do you mean?
J: Well, you know, a white telephone, a grey drum kit, a few green chairs and some small, brown tables.
C: Well, I can't wait to see it!
J: Come over today … Oh … don't forget your sunglasses!

Unit 3B Exercise 5 *page 25*
(A = Andrea, S = Steve)
A: Hi, Steve, it's Andrea.
S: Hello, Andrea. How are you?
A: Fine, thanks. Can I put in an order, please?
S: Of course. Just a moment. Right. What would you like?
A: OK, shirts first. 20 silk shirts in green.
S: OK. They're £29.99 each.
A: Yes. Then jackets. Two black leather jackets. I think they're £110.
S: No, they're 99 now.
A: 10 jumpers – wool. The blue and red ones at £18.
S: 10? OK.
A: 24 pairs of blue denim jeans. And 6 pairs of the white cotton trousers.
S: Right. The jeans are, let me see, £16.80 each, and the trousers are £21.50. OK?
A: That's it.
S: Thanks for the order. Speak to you soon, Andrea. Bye.
A: Bye.

Unit 4A Exercise 5 *page 31*
(A = interviewer, B = interviewee)
A: So, let me ask you a few questions about your skills. Can you type?
B: Yes, I can – on a word processor. I can type about 60 words a minute.
A: OK. What about languages?
B: Well, I'm bilingual in French and English. My father is French but I went to school in London and I can speak some Spanish and a little German.
A: Oh, that's good. How is your written Spanish?
B: Er, not very good, really. I can't write business letters, for example, but, of course, I can learn …
A: Right. Have you got any other skills that you want to tell me about? Skills that are useful if you work for a newspaper?
B: Well, I can drive. I've got an international licence. And I think I'm good with people, I can talk to anyone.
A: OK, good. What about interests? What do you like doing in your spare time?
B: First of all sports. I enjoy skiing. I go most weekends in the winter but in the summer I play tennis. Then … what else … I like reading, of course. I read novels all the time – mostly modern novels. And I play the piano in a jazz band.
A: Do you like playing in front of people?
B: Oh yes. I love it.
A: Why?
B: Because it's … exciting. When you play well and people enjoy it, it's a wonderful feeling.

Unit 4C Exercise 4 *page 35*

A: OK. That's all I want to ask you. Would you like to ask me anything?
B: Oh, yes, I do have one or two questions.
A: Right.
B: Can I ask about the salary first?
A: It's 150,000 francs a year. So that's about 12,500 a month.
B: Twelve thousand five hundred ... right, thank you. And can I ask about holidays too?
A: You get four weeks holiday. People usually take one week at Christmas, one week at Easter and two in the summer.
B: Right, thanks. And the hours: can you tell me about the working hours?
A: Well, this is a daily newspaper. The offices never close. There's always someone at work. But the normal hours in the Advertising Department are nine to five.
B: Monday to Friday?
A: Yes. But sometimes people work in the evenings and at weekends when there's a problem.
B: I see.
A: Is there anything else?
B: Er, no, I don't think so.
A: Right! Well, thank you for coming to the interview. It's been very interesting to meet you ...

Unit 5A Exercise 4 *page 39*
(I = interviewer, A = Agnieszka)
I: What's the structure of the company?
A: Er, well our boss is English, and he's the General Manager. Then we have the Deputy General Manager and he's Polish. And then below him, we have the Group Directors, and they're two young talented Polish people, and then we have managers, Account Managers ... and then Account Executives, and then we have all the support staff like secretaries and executive secretaries.

Unit 5A Exercise 7 *page 39*
I'm a receptionist. There are two of us on the front desk. Above me there is an Office Manager. He's also responsible for all the secretaries. There are about six secretaries. Then there is the Administration Manager. She's one of four managers, and above them is the Director.

Unit 5B Exercise 4 *page 40*
a It's on the first floor.
b It's on the fifth floor.
c It's on the fourth floor.
d It's on the eleventh floor.
e It's on the seventh floor.
f It's on the third floor.
g It's on the second floor.
h It's in the basement.

Unit 5B Exercise 6 *page 40*
first second third fourth fifth sixth seventh eighth ninth tenth eleventh twelfth

Unit 5B Exercise 9 *page 41*
1 A: Where's the Ministry of Information?
   B: It's behind the station.
2 A: Is this the way to the Inter-fashion office?
   B: Yes. It's near the hospital.
3 A: Where's Jet Travel?
   B: It's next door to the secondary school.
4 A: Excuse me. Where's the Euro Exports office?
   B: It's over there, opposite the church.
5 A: Where's Pan Music?
   B: It's round the corner from the post office.
6 A: Where are the Britinvest offices?
   B: They're in the same building as Lloyds Bank.
7 A: How do I get to National Metals?
   B: It's in the same street as the station, above a restaurant.

Unit 5C Exercise 2 *page 42*
a A: What do you want?
   B: Can I help you?
b A: Fill in the visitor's book.
   B: Can you fill in the visitor's book, please?
c A: Can I have your name?
   B: Name?
d A: Sit down for a moment.
   B: Would you take a seat for a moment?

Unit 5C Exercise 4 *page 43*
(R = receptionist, V= visitor)
R: Good afternoon. Can I help you?
V: Er ... yes. I've got an appointment with Mrs Major at 2.30.
R: Can I take your name, please?
V: Yes, It's Paul Symons – S-Y-M-O-N-S.
R: And which company are you from, Mr Symons?
V: Er ... York Computers.
R: Right. Just a moment, please. (*on the phone*) Mrs Major, Mr Symons from York Computers is here to see you. Yes. OK.
   Right. Can you fill in the visitor's book, please, Mr Symons?
V: Certainly.

Unit 5C Exercise 7 *page 43*
(R = receptionist, V = visitor)
1 R: Good morning. It's Mrs Martelli, isn't it?
   V: That's right. Can I see Mrs Major please?
   R: Let me see ... Ah, yes.She's free in 15 minutes. Can I take your coat?
2 R: Good morning.
   V: Good morning. Is Mrs Smith in her office?
   R: No, I'm afraid she's out. Can I take a message?
   V: Yes, it's Mr Allouit. Can you tell her I can't meet her tomorrow? Is she free for lunch next Thursday, do you know? 1.30?
   R: I'm sorry, I don't know. I'll ask her to telephone you.
   V: I'm not in the office this afternoon. Perhaps she can speak to my secretary.
   R: Certainly.
3 R: Good afternoon. Can I help you?
   V: Yes, I'm here to collect some papers. The name's Fry, Mrs Fry.
   R: Ah, yes. Here you are.

Unit 6A Exercise 1 *page 46*
1 Er, this is Paul Carlson from BritPol. Industries for Mr Nowakowski at 5.00 p.m. on Thursday. I'll ring again tomorrow. Thank you.

2 Thank you. She has meetings this afternoon and ... yes, she's out of the office tomorrow morning. She's here from about three o'clock. Could Ms Dymek ring after that?

3 I'm afraid he isn't here at the moment, but when he comes in I'll ask him to ring you immediately.

Unit 6A Exercise 2 *page 46*
(R = receptionist, C = caller)
R: Good morning, Hanson. Can I help you?
C: Good morning. My name's Magda Kranz. I'd like to speak to someone about a job in the Sales Department, please.
R: Just a moment. I'll put you through to the Sales Manager, Mrs Hughes.
C: Thank you very much.
R: I'm sorry, Mrs Hughes is in a meeting, then she's out of the office until tomorrow. Would you like to leave a message, or perhaps write to her?
C: Er ... no, I'll call her tomorrow.
R: All right. I'll tell her. Goodbye.
C: Goodbye

Unit 6B Exercise 3 *page 48*
(C = caller, R = receptionist, S = secretary)
a R: Tall Orders. Can I help you?
   C: Good morning. Could I speak to John Penright, please?
   R: Just a moment, I'll connect you to his secretary.
b S: Mr Penright's office. Gary speaking.
   C: Good morning. This is Tony Bates of Cagny Distribution. I'd like a word with Mr Penright about our new contract. Is Mr Penright there?
   S: Yes he is, I'll put you through.

Unit 6B Exercise 5 *page 48*
(C = caller, R = receptionist)
a C: Can I speak to James West, please?
   R: I'm afraid he isn't here at the moment.
b C: Is Mr West there, please?
   R: Yes, but he's in a meeting until twelve thirty.
c C: Could I speak to Mr West?
   R: Yes, just a moment, please.
d C: Is James West in his office?
   R: I'm not sure – I'll just check.
e C: Can I speak to Mr West, please?
   R: Certainly. I'll put you through.
f C: I'd like to speak to James West, please.
   R: I'm sorry, he isn't in the office.

Unit 6C Exercise 5 *page 51*
(S = secretary, C = caller)
S: Reilly Associates. Good afternoon.
C: Oh, hello. This is Marc Bedouelle. Could I speak to Mrs Reilly, please?
S: I'm afraid she's in a meeting, Mr Bedouelle.

C: Well, can I make an appointment for Mr Clerc to see her later this afternoon? Is she free at half past three?

S: No, I'm sorry. She isn't in the office until four. Is four thirty convenient?

C: Yes … yes, that's fine. Thank you.

S: Goodbye.

Unit 6C Exercise 7 *page 51*
This is Susan Reilly of Reilly Associates for Mr Ellison. I'm so sorry I missed the meeting yesterday, but there was a fire in the office. Could I make another appointment? Any time on Monday or Tuesday is fine. My new, temporary number is 0181 634 8877. Thank you.

Unit 7A Exercise 2 *page 54*
(B = boss, S = secretary)

B: Right, I leave Warsaw on April 2nd and I've got to be back in the office on April 18th or before. Can you book flights for me, please?

S: Certainly. So you want to leave on the 2nd …

B: Yes. Now, I'm visiting a number of Burson-Marsteller offices in Europe.

S: Right.

B: I've got to be in London for three days and … let me see … Madrid for two.

S: Two days in Madrid.

B: Yes – and also in Spain, I've got to visit the Barcelona office.

S: How many days there?

B: Oh, I think two days will be OK in Barcelona.

S: OK.

B: The others are Frankfurt and Budapest. Three days in Frankfurt and four in Budapest.

S: Budapest … four days. OK.

B: That's it. Can you arrange hotels for me too?

S: Yes, sure. And what about the meetings?

B: I'll give you a list of people I've got to see and perhaps you can call them and arrange times?

S: Right. I'll start now.

B: Thanks very much.

Unit 7A Exercise 6 *page 55*

A: Hi Jackie, how are you?

B: Fine thanks. And you?

A: Not too bad. Busy as always.

B: Yes … I know what you mean.

A: I'm phoning to arrange some meetings for Ms Pawlowska when she's in London. She'd like to see Mr Elliott.

B: Right. When is she in London?

A: From April 9th to the 11th.

B: OK. Let me check Mr Elliott's diary. Now then … April 9th … that's a Monday … he's busy in the morning … how about 3 o'clock on Monday afternoon?

A: No … I'm afraid Ms Pawlowska's in another meeting then. She's free on Tuesday morning.

B: Is she free all morning?

A: Yes.

B: OK. Mr Elliott can see her at 10.30 – but he's only free for an hour.

A: That's fine.

B: OK then … Tuesday April 10th at 10.30 … here in his office.

A: Fine … thanks. Nice to speak to you.

B: You too. Bye …

A: Goodbye Jackie.

Unit 7C Exercise 2 *page 58*
(R = receptionist, S = secretary)

R: Royal Hotel. Can I help you?

S: Oh, hello. I'd like to book a room, please.

R: OK. For which days?

S: Er … August 23rd. He's arriving on the 23rd and leaving on the 24th. Just one night.

R: Arriving on August 23rd and leaving on the 24th.

S: That's right.

R: And the name, please?

S: Mr Swallow

R: Can you spell that, please.

S: S-W-A-L-L-O-W.

R: And the initials?

S: Er … J.

R: Mr J. Swallow.

S: Yes.

R: And the company name?

S: The company name is Berber. B-E-R-B-E-R.

R: Berber. OK. What kind of room would you like?

S: Er – a single with a bathroom.

R: Single … with bath. Fine.

S: Can you give us a company discount?

R: Certainly. Our company discount is 20 per cent.

S: OK. So how much is the room?

R: One hundred and twenty dollars plus tax.

S: That's fine.

R: OK. Let me check the details again. That's a single room with bath for Mr J.Swallow. He's arriving on August 23rd and leaving on August 24th.

S: That's right.

R: Fine. Could you send me a fax to confirm Mr Swallow's reservation, please?

S: Certainly. Who shall I send it to?

R: Send it to me. My name's Ms Hartmann. H-A-R-T-M-A-N-N.

S: Right.

R: Thank you for calling.

S: Thanks for your help. Goodbye.

R: Bye.

Unit 8A Exercise 2 *page 62*
Agnieszka Whelan is describing a publicity event for a satellite television company called FilmNet.
We put a very, very big monkey, which was like a King Kong, on top of the Palace of Culture for two days, and it was, it was about twenty metres tall … and it did create a lot of interest – I mean there were people who thought it was ugly and there were people who thought it was a really great idea, but that's what we wanted … we didn't want everybody to say, 'This is wonderful', we just wanted people to see it and start asking questions … who put it there and why? And it was there for two days and … erm … on the last day at night we had a big party for about 600 people and …er… we got famous faces like people from

television, from theatre, from the movies and … er … a lot of TV presenters and a lot of business contacts for FilmNet, for our clients … And of course we had a lot of food and a lot of champagne and music.

Unit 9A Exercise 8b *page 71*
two point six per cent
four point two per cent
five point nine per cent
eight point six per cent
eight point seven per cent
eleven point five per cent

Unit 9B Exercise 5 *page 73*

A: You have a lot of parties and receptions here at PLT, don't you? Who organises them?

B: David, in Public Relations. He's over there in the brown suit.

A: Oh, yes. Who does he work with?

B: He's got a small team of assistants. You know Mary, don't you?

A: Yes. What does she do?

B: She invites major clients – like yourself. That's just a routine task, really.

A: Who invites the other guests, then? David?

B: Yes, he decides which company staff attend, and he identifies useful public figures – politicians, and so on.

A: Right. What brings them here – the politicians, I mean?

B: Oh, good food, a lot to drink. Perhaps the hope of a job after politics?

Unit 10A Exercise 5b *page 79*

A: So how is this packaging done?

B: First each copier is wrapped in plastic and packed in polystyrene to protect it. Then the box is made and the copier is put in it. Next, the manuals and so on are added to the box and the box is closed and sealed. It is loaded onto a truck and when the truck is full the copiers are transported to a distributor so that the copiers reach the customer as soon as possible.

Unit 11A Exercise 2 *page 86*
(V = Véronique, Y = Yveline)
V: I hate it when you call a person and the first thing you say is about business. I always like to say something personal first, you know: What did you do last weekend? Did you go out? What was that film like? etc. etc., because I know them. And then after that I talk about business. Actually, it's much better this way. I mean, it's better for business, because when you are friendly with people, it's much easier to get what you want from them – I mean on the business side. If I want someone to help me with a problem at work, it's much easier if I talk about personal things first. I think so, anyway.

Y: It's a funny thing, really. When I call people in our other offices abroad, if they are French, I speak to them in French. If I know they are German, I speak to them in German. But I only use that language for chatting – you know, at the beginning of the conversation: How are you? How's everything going? You know. But as soon as we start to talk about business, we both change to English because English is the language of the company and we automatically use English to talk about work things. I suppose it's strange to other people, but for us it's natural.

Unit 11B Exercise 1d *page 88*
a A: Good afternoon. Is that Mrs Pane's office?
 B: Yes, it is. I'm her new assistant, Tom Drysdale. Her last assistant left to have a baby …
 A: I'd just like to cancel my appointment tomorrow. The name's Foyle. Val Foyle.
 B: Tomorrow … Let's see. What's the date tomorrow? Oh yes, here we are. Mrs Foyle. Actually, Mrs Pane will be pleased about that, because she wants to go to the hairdresser, and …
 A: Right. I'll telephone to make another appointment. Thank you.
 B: Goodbye.

b A: Good morning. This is Paul Darwin. Am I speaking to Mr Bellow's assistant?
 B: That's right.
 A: I see. Well, could I speak to Mr Bellow, please?
 B: He's not here.
 A: So when will he be in the office, then?
 B: At about five o'clock.
 A: Thank you.

c A: Hello, I'm phoning from Clearview Plastics. I'd like to arrange a meeting with Ms Lyle, please. She wants to see me about a new contract.
 B: Certainly. Could you give me your name, please?
 A: It's Patrick Bush.
 B: Right, Mr Bush. Would next Tuesday be convenient? At eleven o'clock?
 A: Yes, that's fine. Thank you very much.
 B: Thank you, Mr Bush. Goodbye.

Unit 12B Exercise 7 *page 97*
A: It's really nice to hear from you after all this time.
B: How are things? What are you doing these days?
A: Oh, things aren't so good really …
B: Oh, I'm sorry to hear that, Paul. Why not? What's wrong?
A: Well, I lost my job about two years ago and I just can't get another one. It's really difficult.
B: You were a computer programmer, weren't you?
A: Yes, that's right, but the company closed. I applied for other jobs but … well, you know, there just aren't many around. So now I'm unemployed. I've got some freelance work – I've got a few contacts – but I want to get a proper job. I need to earn more.
B: What would you like to do?

A: Well, of course I'd like to stay in computing. The trouble is that the technology changes very fast and I'm out of touch.
B: Yes … What about doing a course? You know, to retrain.
A: Yes, I am looking for a course for the summer. The problem's the cost. We'll see. Anyway, what about you?

Unit 12C Exercise 2 *page 98*
(I = interviewer, L = Liana)
I: Why is English taught at ELEA?
L: Because it is the language that people need to use in international communication, whether it be over the telephone or face-to-face or for travel purposes … er … the reason why other people are studying languages other than English is that they go to that country, for example for a specific German contract.

Unit 12C Exercise 5 *page 99*
(I = interviewer, L = Liana)
I: What are the particular needs of secretarial staff?
L: Secretaries mainly need to improve their English on the telephone. The telephone is a big problem because they cannot see the person. They can ask for the questions to be repeated over the telephone, but often it's difficult to hear over the telephone: the voice isn't clear, there's crackle … and so the telephone, I think, is the biggest problem generally – and the other problem is face-to-face conversation.
I: But what about speaking on the telephone? What advice do you give?
L: We tell students that they need to get a message across, and not to worry if all of the verbs are not 100% correct, but to get the message across in the best way they can …

Project 1:
On the answerphone *page 102*
A
Oh … hello. I'm phoning to ask for a copy of your new catalogue. Could you send me one as soon as possible, please? My name is Pritchard … P-R-I-T-C-H-A-R-D … and I'm at 138 Bethnal Street … that's B-E-T-H-N-A-L … London SE4 2JB. Thanks.
B
Er … this is a message for Lorna Davies. I've got a meeting with her on Tuesday at 2.00 p.m. My name's David Long. I'm afraid I have to cancel the meeting: something urgent has come up. Could we arrange another time? I'm free on … let me see … Wednesday between 10.00 a.m. and midday. Or any time on Friday afternoon. Could you call my secretary and let her know if one of these times is OK? Again, my apologies.
C
Hello Gillian, this is Lorna. I'm afraid I'm going to be a little late tomorrow morning. Could you fax Sally Thomas and change our meeting from 10.30 to 11.30? Thanks. Please give her my apologies.

D
Oh, this is ABC Computers. Just to let you know that our computer technician will be with you tomorrow, that's Tuesday, at about two o'clock. Thanks. Goodbye.
E
Oh … an answerphone … er … I wanted to speak to Bill Davies … er … well, it doesn't matter … I'll call again in the morning.
F
I'm phoning about the job advertisement for a secretary. Could you send me an application form and any other information, please? My name's E. Blake … B-L-A-K-E … and I'm at 45, Stratton Road … S-T-R-A-T-T-O-N … Bristol BS4 3AH. Thanks very much.
G
Oh dear … er … I need to speak to Lorna Davies urgently. Could she please telephone as soon as she arrives in the office tomorrow morning? It's Monday now, ten past six. I'm Andrew Potter and she can call me on 653917.
H
This is RJ Deliveries. Our driver tried to deliver a package to you this afternoon but discovered that you have moved. Could you please fax details of your new address and we can then deliver immediately. Our fax number is 387 4002. Thanks.

Unit 13A Exercise 2 *page104*
The Herald Tribune is the only truly international daily newspaper and we print and sell it all over the world. Er, our biggest market is Europe, of course, where 68% of the papers are sold. Within Europe, France is the biggest country market, with Germany, Britain and Switzerland also very important. We also have large sales in the Asia / Pacific area. We sold an average of over 43,000 there last year: 23% of our total circulation.
Then there are the Americas – that's the States, Canada, Latin America and the Caribbean – we call that area the Americas. We sold 12,303 there last year: 6% of the circulation.
We sell a little more than three and a half thousand in the Middle East – that's all the Arab countries including North Africa. That area takes about 2% of our daily sales, and our smallest market is the Sub-Saharan area of Africa where we sell about one and a half thousand.

Unit 13C Exercise 6 *page 109*
a 28.4 b 7.12 c 65% d 7/12
e 13% f 1/3 g 0.13 h 82.4

Unit 14C Exercise 1 *page 116*
(I = interviewer, G = Gerald)
I: So, Gerald, can you tell me about your educational background, please?
G: Yes, certainly. The last course I did was at Swansea College of Further Education. I was there from 1991 to 1992 and I left with a Diploma in Marketing.
I: A Diploma in Marketing. Right …
G: And before that I passed A levels in Business Studies and German.
I: I see. What grades did you get for your A levels?

G: Er … I got a B in Business Studies and a C in German.

I: Right … and what about GCSE results? How many did you pass?

G: Er … eight. I got two As – in Business Studies and German; 3 Bs – in Geography, History and Art; and three Cs. The three Cs were in Maths, Chemistry and … what was the other … oh yes, Music.

I: As in Business Studies and German …

G: Yes, that's right …

I: Bs in Geography, History and …

G: Art.

I: And Cs in …

G: Maths, Chemistry and Music.

I: OK. Can we turn to your previous employment now? Tell me about the jobs you've had since you left college.

G: Well, I'm Personal Assistant to the Sales Director of a company called Short Breaks. We sell short holidays – usually four or five days – in Britain and Europe. I've been with Short Breaks for three years: since 1994.

I: So did you work in Britain all the time?

G: Most of the time. But I have visited a lot of the places where we have our holidays – Munich, Prague, Budapest, Paris.

I: That sounds good. So why do you want to leave?

G: Well, I think it's because I've done everything. I've worked in all the departments of the company. It's been very enjoyable and interesting but there's nothing new for me to do there now.

I: Yes, I can understand that. And before Short Breaks? Where were you then?

G: From the time I left college in July 1992 until I started at Short Breaks in March 1994, I worked for a hotel company called The Three Towers Group.

I: The Three Towers Group. Yes, I've heard of them … and what did you do for them?

G: I was a secretary. I worked with computers a lot: I had to produce figures for the whole group on the numbers of guests in all the hotels every week. I also helped to write questionnaires for guests: to collect information about them, and to build an address list.

I: I see. And did you enjoy that job?

G: Yes. It gave me an opportunity to learn about computers and …

Unit 15A Exercise 2 *page 120*
Part 1

I am an Executive Secretary or Personal Assistant. I work for the head of international advertising here at the Herald Tribune. I guess my job … the job of any Personal Assistant is to help our boss in whatever way he or she needs it. I do all the routine things: lots of internal paperwork. I arrange his agenda, I make all his arrangements, book his flights and hotels. I take dictation. I take all his phone calls … and I try to deal with them myself. The idea is to give my boss the time to do the really important things in his job.

Part 2

So of course, you have to be very well-organised. And you have to be very diplomatic with people. But the most important quality an assistant needs is: you have to be helpful. You must always say, 'Yes it's possible!' If there's a problem, try to find a way around it. You've made something possible. And in any job with an international company you have to speak languages and get to know the country you're working in. I'm from Venezuela and I speak three languages fluently. Spanish is my mother tongue; then I speak English and French. My boss is British.

Unit 15A Exercise 7 *page 121*
(B = boss, S = secretary)

B: Dear Brian – comma – new paragraph – heading – capital letters, travel. I'm arriving on Sunday – full stop. My flight details are – colon – BA 457 (*pause*) comma.
(*pause*) Arriving Dublin 9.30 – open brackets – if it's not late – exclamation mark, close brackets. Full stop. (*pause*) Can you meet me with a hire car – dash – nothing too expensive – question mark.

S: Could you speak a little more slowly?

B: Yes, OK. New paragraph – heading, HOTEL.

S: Has that got capital letters?

B: Hotel? Yes. OK? I'd like to stay at Polansky's again – semi-colon.

S: Can you spell that, please?

B: Polansky's? P-O-L-A-N-S-K-Y – apostrophe – S. Put that in inverted commas.

S: OK.

B: It was fine last time – full stop. (*pause*) But please make sure it's a quiet room, full stop. I look forward …

S: Is this a new paragraph?

B: Er … yes. I look forward to seeing you again (*pause*) and hearing about (*pause*) developments in (*pause*) the Irish market, full stop.

Unit 16A Exercise 3 *page 129*
Part 1

There are two kinds of advertising supplement. The first kind is a subject supplement. It's international. We choose a subject, for example, finance, banking, education, something like that, and we sell advertising to companies in that business. The second kind is a country supplement – so it's a national report – and it can be about a country anywhere in the world: Germany, Bangladesh, South Africa, Brazil … Then we sell advertisements to any companies in that country: the type of business is not important.

Part 2

It's very easy when it's a country report because you just deal with one market – in English, except when the country is France. I call the rep in that country and I ask him how many pages he can sell. If he thinks he can sell a lot I tell him to go ahead. But when a supplement is international, I have to speak to all our reps around the world. So I call every office in every market and I ask if they think they can sell the subject. They tell me that they can sell … maybe half a page. Sometimes they say that it's a problem and they want to know if they can have more time. Sometimes – not very often – they say it's a difficult subject for their market.

Unit 16A Exercise 6 *page 129*
(R = rep, A = assistant, V = Véronique)

R: I can sell about half a page on banking.

A: He says he can sell about half a page on banking.

V: Ask him if he can sell it before next week.

A: Can you sell it before next week?

R: I think I need more time.

A: He says he needs more time.

V: How much more time?

A: Véronique wants to know how much more time.

R: I can do it in two weeks.

A: He says he can do it in two weeks.

V: That's fine.

A: Véronique says that's fine.

Unit 16C Exercise 2 *page 132*

The next stage is that I get the orders for adverts from the reps. They fax them to me here in Paris. I do the advertising layout and of course many advertisers ask for a specific position for their ad. So I take the page and I do the page layout – it's like a puzzle.
When I have done the advertising layout I give it to the person who's going to do the production layout. That person puts the ads with the article, illustrations and anything else that has to go in the section.